EXCEPTIONAL NOT EXPECTED

An Ordinary Woman's Guide to Living an Empowered Life

Author

Yvonne Ellis

Bible scripture Quotations are taken from the New King James Version of the Bible.

www.yemeempowerment.com

Yvonne Ellis/Exceptional Not Expected

ISBN:978-1-9998590-4-6

DEDICATION

Thank you, my Father the Living God, for the gift of ideas, and the skills, talents, experiences, hope and strength you have given me to live an exceptional life. Through your son Jesus Christ I am living the empowered life you predestined for me.

To my husband Stephen thank you for the idea for this book. Your encouragement and input are appreciated. I love you.

My darling Jada. You continue to inspire me as a mother. I love you dearly.

Tennika I will always love you.

To anyone that wants something different in life it is never too late to achieve it. This book is for you.

Contents

Introduction

It feels like it has taken me a lifetime (well, over twenty years) for me to finally be at a place where I am living the life I want. It has been a life-changing and transformative journey. I have learned to adapt my way of thinking as I overcame certain obstacles; such as: lies, low confidence, and low self-esteem. It took a lot of hard work; self-reflection, therapy – and courage, to lay hold of what was mine in the first place – the right to live my life to its full capacity and purpose, without feeling I needed *permission* to do so, because I came from disadvantaged beginnings.

However, to be exceptional and not expected, I first had to work my way through the dross and dirt left behind from childhood trauma. In addition, I had to unlearn toxic habits and change my mindset. Most importantly, I had to change the way I viewed myself; my capabilities, my potential, and my value. After working through an array of different and difficult challenges, tests and trials, I finally started the journey to live the life I never thought possible, at the grand age of thirty-five years old.

My transformational journey and my (then) fourteen-year-old daughter's school report, served as the inspiration to write this book. Her report listed all the subjects she had undertaken. The teacher marked her comprehension of each subject, graded as follows: expected (basically means as predicted), and exceptional (exceeded expectations). This was an epiphany moment for me and an accurate representation of how I was living my life a decade ago – and from my observations on how many people live their lives today. So, when I decided to write this book *Exceptional Not Expected: An ordinary woman's guide to living an empowered life*, it was an opportunity to share with you, the reader, that you can live the life you want at any age, despite the challenges, tests, and trials that we encounter in this complicated and beautiful experience called life.

Let me ask you a question: How many of you, like me, have always done what is expected, predicted, or determined by people, life, or circumstances? For instance, turning up every day to a job you do not want to do because of responsibilities, just giving minimal effort (what is expected) because the things you are doing don't inspire you to do or want more; and those around us – whether in work, family or our community – don't encourage us to strive for more, because what they expect from you is based on what they *see* you do, not on your potential or promise? Some of us (and I'm guessing you are one of them) want to be exceptional. We know we are capable of great things, but our surroundings, current circumstances, social circle, negative self-talk, and other hindrances stop us from daring to explore our true potential. Consequently, we do what is expected of us, not what we believe in ourselves.

And herein lies the problem. Because you and I were not created by the Living God to live sub-par lives, ticking other people's boxes, limited by ourselves or the expectations of society on how we should live our lives. We are created in the image of God, and He has designed and assigned each of us a specific and unique purpose to fulfil. Until we discover and tap into it, we will always live life to the standard of 'expected' and not 'exceptional'. In turn, we will have very little to show for a life meant to be lived to the full.

So, what does it mean to live 'exceptional' and not 'expected'? And how does it show up in a person's life? Well, it comprises different things. It involves making intentional choices and decisions. It means taking action to undertake a journey of self-improvement and personal development. It's about discovering your God-given purpose, through a relationship with God and living your life tailored to it. It involves embracing you authentically and holding on to you in the process of personal change; courageously breaking out of the boxes, barriers, stereotypes, and constraints that life, people, and circumstances have you hemmed in. And of course, daring to be different and live differently through transforming your mindset. And do you know what? the wonderful thing about living exceptionally and not expected? *anyone can do it*. You don't have to be rich, famous, or considered important in the eyes of others; you just have to make up your mind that this is the standard by which you want to live your life – you have to *want* it. To be exceptional is all about desiring to live an empowered life to a high standard of excellence, with vision, purpose, and intention. To acquire it is a journey of sacrifice, self-discovery, courage, and knowledge; it's about living true to who you are uniquely called to be.

It took me a long time to understand and walk in the belief that I am exceptional. And yes, I boldly claim the term for myself. I have earned every right to, and, in all things, I give the glory to Jesus Christ to whom all honour is due. It is a feat that could only (in my experience) be achieved through Jesus Christ, who empowered me to not only survive, but thrive in the face of trauma and adversity, and defy the odds people and society expected from someone of my background.

In this book, I share with you my advice, wisdom, tips, knowledge, encouragement, and insight, from lessons learned whilst going through different life experiences and overcoming challenges. It is empowering knowledge that I have shared in part through blogs, podcasts, social media posts, and countless journal notes I kept over the years, as well as new reflections on my current life journey. The life topics covered in this book are things that I have personally experienced, which I have transformed into tips and 'how-to' steps, to help you make a positive life change. Some of the entries are long, while others are short and to the point. Nonetheless, all that I share from my journey has brought me personal success. Additionally, throughout the book, I share quotes that I created to empower, encourage, and inspire you. The beauty of this book is that you can dip in and out when you want, and you can go directly to a subject matter for the situation you are facing. I also share a biblical word to encourage you.

Even though I see myself as exceptional, I am no different to you. I am an ordinary woman, that took advantage of situations and opportunities to develop and help me live the best life possible. As a result, I am now doing amazing things. I started from where I was with what I had. I made changes – and you can too!

Yvonne x

Break
Limitations Have
Expectations

Accept and Love You

The main thing you will need to be exceptional and not expected, is to accept and love you. I know that for many people this is not easy to do. The messages society conveys to us through social media, advertisements, and other visual mediums, is that if we have whatever it is that they are 'selling' us, then it will make us more desirable, better, accepted, and loved. But the truth is; all you need is *you*. Yes, all of you. Your flaws, your unique ways; just you. When you can accept and love yourself for who you are – then you have everything.

I have battled for many years to accept and even like myself. My abuse left me feeling inadequate, less than, incomplete and broken. It resulted in me pursuing unhealthy ways to try and accept myself. I sought validation from others, I focused on my appearance, anything to try and seek self-love. However, I didn't realise until I was in my late twenties, that it all starts from within. It meant I had to deal with my brokenness. It meant that instead of rejecting myself because of the shame of my abuse, I had to accept myself exactly how I was. It was not easy, but what I gained from accepting and loving myself as I was, was a sense of peace. I know I am not perfect. I know I am not the most attractive person on the planet – and I know that I am not everyone's cup of tea. However, I know most importantly of all that I am loved by God and that I am fearfully and wonderfully made by the creator of heaven and earth. He knows all the worst things about me and loves me with everlasting love; that is more than enough. Yet at one point in my life, it was not more than enough for me, but taking the step to believe it, until I felt it, gave me reassurance and acceptance about myself. Everything else transcended from that God-given truth. It is still a journey, but I can say that I accept and love who I am.

If you want to be exceptional and not expected, you must first accept yourself and then over time, learn to like and love yourself. If you can do that, the pressure to conform to the pressures of society and the expectations of everyone else will decrease.

If you struggle to accept and love yourself, I would recommend:

Accept the unconditional love of God through his Jesus Christ.

Embrace yourself how you are; in the acknowledgement that you are still a work in progress.

Show yourself grace not condemnation.

The most powerful gift you can give yourself is acceptance and love. If you cannot give yourself that, why would others around you, or those whose validation you are seeking, give that to you? Besides the grace of God, success and contentment in life will flow from this truth; you must be at peace with who you are.

But God demonstrates his own love towards us, in that while we were still sinners, Christ died for us. **Romans 5:8**

Be a Change Agent

To live the empowered life, to be exceptional and not expected, is to aspire to live a life that blesses, empowers, and encourages others. 'A rich life is a life that empowers others' *unknown.*

A while back, I read a book called *Change Agent* by Os Hillman. His book opened my eyes to small-level influence, meaning, at a level that starts with what *I* can do. You see, some people think making a difference, which basically is what a change agent is, means doing a big, noticeable thing, or they are under the impression that you need lots of resources, a large following or support to do it. But you don't need the razzmatazz; you just need the desire and heart to do it.

To be a change agent, means you help others using your skills, talents, or experiences to influence your family, community, or society for the better. Additionally, for me as a Christ follower and a Christian woman, it means using my faith to connect those elements to introduce people to Jesus, through the things he has called me to do. A change agent empowers, encourages, uplifts, and helps other people.

I am a change agent in my family. I encourage my family to live a life pleasing to God and help them find ways to be a person of influence in their school and workplace. My husband and I are change agents in our marriage, as both of us come from unwed homes. By our example, we are influencing our daughter through our commitment to marriage. We hope our decision will set a new direction for future generations of our family. Another way I became a change agent, is by just using my voice to tell my story about childhood sexual abuse. It started with the first book I released, over a decade ago. Then I set up *Daughter Arise*, a non-profit to help others with the same experiences. It has opened doors for me to do inspirational talks, including a TEDx talk, books, and workshops to empower, encourage, educate, and inspire people from different walks of life, and in various professions. What was meant for bad in my life, God has used for good.

To be a change agent, means you can help better the lives of others. You can start to build a legacy that will last after you pass away. Also, it is a wonderful way to be a blessing to others. Here are a few examples of how you can become a change agent:

In your family

Encourage and uplift your family. Help them if they are struggling with bad habits or problems, by seeking solutions to their problems.

Raise awareness

If you have personal experience with an issue – especially something you have overcome – this is valuable information. Try and find a way to use it to help others going through the same thing.

In the workplace

Have you spotted a problem that you can help with? Do you know an easier way to do a task that your colleagues will benefit from? Share the information.

A change agent starts where they are, with what they have. Remember, it is for the benefit of others, and they might not recognise or give you credit for it. However, consider it your gift to the world and don't look for anything in return. Influencing others with kindness and selflessness will bring rewards in ways you never expected.

Give, and it will be given to you: good measure, pressed down, shaken together, and running over will be put into your bosom. For with the same measure that you use, it will be measured back to you. **Luke 6:38**

Be Interested and Invested

Are you interested in where your life is going? Are you invested in where you want to take it? A major sign you are not interested or invested in your life, is that you are just living day to day with no purpose, aim or direction. The things you do are just enough to get by. To get to where you want to go in life, you have got to pay close attention, be interested, and be invested in the small details. You have got to invest the time, effort and sacrifice to get what you want. To be where you want to be.

A major reason people are not interested and invested in their life, is because they find themselves at a point in life where they are doing things they don't want to do. The person who had a dream of starting their own craft business has spent years working in an admin job. With each day that goes by, they feel the dream slipping away. Therefore, what they are currently doing means nothing to them. At one point in my life, I was that person. Childhood trauma and low confidence had me believing there was no point in being interested and invested in life. However, that changed when Jesus saved me, and I discovered my life purpose. Maybe in reading this entry, you find that it somewhat reflects how you feel about your life currently and where you are now. I want you to know that things can change. You can start to be interested and invested in your life by:

Igniting the spark

Find that thing you are passionate about. Maybe it is something you loved in your past, but gave up on long ago. Once you find it, engage in doing it. It doesn't matter how often, as long as you start.

Writing down your goals and dreams

Take yourself out for a coffee and bring a notebook. Write down your goals and dreams. Don't dismiss any of them just because you feel it is impossible or too late. Allow your mind the space to dream. Aim to write down at least one thing on your list. Then plan the steps you will need to achieve it. Don't put a timeframe on it.

Paying attention

What things are causing you to give up? What habits are holding you back? What has caused you to not be interested in your life? Take time to think about it. Once you have identified those hindrances, decide what you are going to do to remove them. You can pour clean water into a dirty tank. Meaning you must remove the distractions that cause you not to be interested or invested in your life, before you can focus on the things you want to fill it with. Investment requires full attention.

Remember, if you are not interested and invested in your life no one else is going to be. Make your life your priority. Live with intention and focus. That is how you will live a quality life.

Be very careful, then how you live not as unwise but as wise. **Ephesians:5v15**

Beware of The Mind Traps

Mind traps are those things that lull you into a false sense of security, which causes you to stop or relax before you reach your goal or achieve your objectives, because you have made progress.

Let me tell you about the mind trap I have fallen into many times concerning weight loss. It has been an up-and-down battle, especially over the last four years. The latest struggle happened during the pandemic. I lost 9 lbs and I had 3 lbs to lose to reach my target weight. I was doing so well; eating right, exercising, and doing intermittent fasting, I was consistent and focused. However, I took my eyes off the prize, and I started eating some unhealthy snacks and before I knew it, I put back on 2lbs. The mind trap that lulled me into a false sense of security, was that as I was losing weight, it wouldn't do much harm to snack – but it nearly caused me to undo all my hard work. And the worst thing is, I don›t even desire to eat like that anymore, it was out of habit.

It was the wakeup that I needed, and it made me aware, that I had a habit of falling into the same mind trap which was linked to emotional eating. I learned that mind traps always seem to catch me when I get comfortable before I reach my goal. Now, through self-awareness, I can spot the net of the mind trap before I am caught in it and make a conscious decision to do something else that does not hinder my progress.

Some signs you are being lulled into a mind trap are:

You move the goalposts of your goal before you reach it.

You enable yourself to short-circuit your goal achievement with excuses.

You are consistent in something then you take a day off... OK... then two, and three. It then becomes a regular occurrence.

Mind traps are induced by many things and can show up to sabotage you with a lack of patience, loss of focus, distractions, and emotional triggers. Also, not regulating your emotions can lead you to do things you don't want to do (i.e., emotional spending). You must keep the bigger picture, the end goal always. Known comfort – the comfort of where you've been used to can also sabotage the place you're trying to get to.

How to deal with mind traps

Be aware of your weaknesses, personal blind spots, emotional triggers and habits.

Have a plan in order to get back on track.

Remind yourself of why you should stay on track; the reward and the achievement of the desired goal.

Hold yourself accountable in the good and bad. Reflect on what is going well – and the things that have not.

Think about what will help you to move forward productively.

When you have a relationship with Jesus Christ, he will give you His Holy Spirit to help and guide you through your mind traps. However, a relationship with Jesus is not a magic wand. It just means that you won't be doing things with your own strength. Renewing and refreshing your mind with information and knowledge from the word of God, the Bible, can help transform your thinking. It is not easy when those thoughts that lead to mind traps arise.

Be aware of your thoughts and recognise when a mind trap is present. And when you recognise their presence, use one of the things you have as a backup plan to deal with it. It does take a while to get used to, but don't give up. Remember, a trap is only a trap if you let it; you have the power to make your mind free.

Do not be conformed to this world but be transformed by the renewing of your mind, that you may prove what is that good and acceptable and perfect will of God. **Romans 12:2**

Bring Your Ideas to Life

I am always capturing my ideas. I have ideas that come to me in bed at night as I'm going to sleep. When that happens, I quickly write them on the notepad app on my phone or on post-it notes (I have boxes full of these notebooks of ideas). I'm an idea-o-holic!

I can tell you from first-hand experience – a lot of good things come from ideas. Everything I have developed, designed and created, started from an idea; my books, podcast, and businesses. At first, I wasn't good at bringing my ideas to reality. But as I grew in self-belief and had the courage to act, it gave me the confidence to openly share and act upon my ideas. The result has been amazing and rewarding.

As is the nature of ideas, some will be successful, and others may fail. But as you grow accustomed to the cycle of bringing your ideas to life, you will embrace the uncertainty as part of the process. Many people get put off by the very idea of acting *upon* their idea, because well, they think nothing will come of it. But what would happen if they captured that idea and dared to act on it?

Have you got an idea? Something you want to do but have not acted on? Or do you have an idea but haven't written it down? I want to tell you that your idea is valuable. You need to bring your idea to life.

It could be the key to opening new opportunities and income. However, a word of caution – don't expect other people to understand your idea, or the vision you have for it. People only usually 'get it' when they see it as reality (even then they still may not).

So, on that note, I want to encourage you. If an idea pops into your head capture it by:

Note it straight away

According to scientists, an idea only stays in your head for five seconds. Apparently, that is the amount of time you have to capture it before it disappears from your memory. Make sure you capture your idea straightaway by writing, recording, or drawing it.

Think positive about your idea

Don't think about whether it has been done already, or if it will or won't work. Think above what you can imagine. Your execution of the idea, may be the one that people understand in a way they never understood before.

Use what you have at hand

Don't worry about expensive equipment, dazzle, and fluffy stuff. All you need is your imagination and a 'can do' attitude to bring your idea to life.

Everything around you started with an idea. The lightbulb you have in the lamp. The computer you work on. Even the selfie stick! Be inspired by the things around you and encouraged by those that have acted on ideas before you.

Write down the revelation and make it plain on tablets so that a herald may run with it. For the revelation awaits an appointed time; it speaks of the end and will not prove false. Though it lingers, wait for it; it will certainly come and will not delay. **Habakkuk 2: 2-3**

Bucket Whatever List

I am probably not the only person who thought a bucket list is something that only dying people do as a kind of 'last wish' list. As a matter-of-fact, Dictionary. com defines the bucket list as *a list of things a person wants to achieve or experience before reaching a certain age or dying*. However, the bucket list is also known by a variety of names; life list, dream list, my life must-do's, life plan, things to conquer, and life aspiration list. If you don't feel comfortable calling your list a bucket list, you can call it whatever you want if it is a collection of your goals, dreams, and aspirations!

Every year, for as long as I can remember, I have made a goal list (that's what I call mine) of things that I want to achieve. Usually, it is a mix of personal, financial, and family-oriented things I would like to achieve. Sometimes my list is sectioned into one, five, and ten-year goals. As a visual representation of my goals, dreams, and aspirations I created a vision board, which is a collection of pictures and words for different things I want to achieve. Of course, time permitting, some things I achieve while others I fall short of, but it is not something that causes disappointment; rather it encourages me to continue to explore if my goals can be achieved.

It is nice to have things to work towards and to look forward to; goals, dreams and aspirations provide that. It creates a sense of hope, anticipation, and excitement. If you haven't created a list before for your goals, dreams, or aspirations, I want to share with you some simple ideas to get you started:

What should be your list

You should include things that take you outside your comfort zone. A simple way to incorporate this element is through new experiences. Don't dismiss anything as too difficult, or too challenging. Try and be open-minded. The key thing to consider is what it means to you? Will it make you feel a sense of accomplishment or achievement? Work on your list from this viewpoint and then it will inspire you to think about how you can achieve it.

Find inspiration

Visit your favourite places. Think about some of your favourite memories; times when you did something exciting or different. Search event listing sites such as *meet up* and *Eventbrite,* if there is something on your list that you want to do but lack the courage or confidence to do by yourself. Write what inspires you and try and incorporate it into your list.

Decide your list

You can make your list as short or long as you want, but don't set yourself up to fail. Bear in mind you want to include some quick wins to encourage you through the year. I would suggest a list of one to three things to start with. This will take into account any work, family, resources and limited fund constraints. Also, you need to consider what season you are attempting to accomplish goals in. If it is an outside goal, you may have to wait until the weather is warmer. That means you might be waiting until mid-year to start.

Create your list

As mentioned, you can name your list what you want. You can create your list using a notepad phone app, a notebook, or a Word document, or use online graphic templates from websites such as Canva or iWish – a phone app designed to help you with making a list. If you are feeling creative, you can make a visual representation by using old magazines and a piece of card to create a vision board.

Write your list

Your list should contain things that inspire you. It should be meaningful to you, with a mixture of different areas of your life; financial, family, and personal. Also, I would suggest maybe something to bless others. However, it should not be a list of chores or outstanding tasks that need to be done. You can make a list for that at any time!

You can also create a list of things you want to do before a certain age (things to do before thirty, or forty, or a seasonal list. Or things you want to do in the summer, or Christmas).

Remember, that in creating whatever list you choose, it is to enable you to live an empowered life. Really embrace it as your own and create it with the intention in mind that these are the things you want to do. Have fun doing it!

Delight yourself also in the lord, and he shall give you the desires of your heart. **Psalm 37:4**

Celebrate the Wins and Things

It is easy to focus on the things that haven't or didn't happen, especially when you look at all the plans you have for an upcoming year, only to find at the end of the year, things didn't transpire in the way you had hoped. However, I want to encourage you to celebrate the wins and things that *did* happen.

For example, 2020 was a year to remember. Even though the pandemic caused some chaos in my life, great things emerged to be celebrated. My first book *Daughter Arise* turned ten years old in October. I won two awards (Women Appreciating Women and best Small Enterprise Awards for my non-profit Daughter Arise). I created successful online events and won new contracts for my business YEME Empowerment. And personally, I turned a corner in some challenges I struggled with. But would you believe, I nearly overlooked my achievements because I was distracted by what went wrong with that year and because I have a habit of moving on to the next thing! Besides not celebrating the big victories, I had a habit of overlooking the small, everyday ones too. I am ambitious (nothing wrong with that!) and I like to focus on my goals. But I realised this needs to be balanced out with reflection, appreciation, and celebration. So, I decided to make the celebration a part of my journey, by treating myself on occasion. Sometimes I go out for coffee and scrumptious cake or take myself out for a fancy lunch. Or have a glass of prosecco in my home office whilst listening to smooth jazz. What I realised is, it is good to work hard, but equally important to recognise and celebrate your hard work and accomplishments.

I love to spend time at the end of each year reflecting on previous entries in my journal. It serves as a powerful reminder that I have many reasons to celebrate. I remember reading somewhere a while ago, that success is the journey, not the destination. This means we need to pause at times, smell the flowers and enjoy the moment. Whether small, big, personal, private, or public – all achievements matter. If you struggle with celebrating your wins, I want to encourage you to:

Acknowledge your achievements no matter how big or small

Keep a record (journal, gratitude, or milestone jar) so you can go back and reflect on those special moments. Write down how it felt to achieve it.

Appreciate your win

It could be that you overcame depression or that you still have a job. Maybe you gained a different perspective on something you once thought was negative. Whatever your wins and things, recognise and *celebrate* them. For it is in appreciating and celebrating the small things that the big victories will taste sweeter.

Celebrate

Do something you love. It does not have to cost money. If it is something that is rewarding to you, do it and enjoy it.

This is the day which the Lord has made; Let us rejoice and be glad in it. **Psalm 118:24**

Commit to Consistency

What do you think is the key to success? Some people say hard work... In part that is true. Others argue that it is not what you know, but who you know; meaning who you are connected to. I agree that in certain circles, success through connections is a thing. Others may say sacrifice, dedication, and a plan, all of these are important ingredients in the success recipe.

But what if I told you, consistency is the key to success? I know; it doesn't sound glamorous or attractive. Out of all the things people think are key to success, consistency sounds boring and repetitive. However, repetition, aka: consistency, is something success attracts. I want to share something bizarre, funny, and true with you about consistency. Admittedly, I only realised this on reflection of my efforts that it was true.

Consistency is a tortoise and God impressed upon me to become like one. No, of course, I can't change *into* one, but I can develop the characteristics of one. So, with that thought in mind, I searched the internet and found the story of the tortoise and the hare, the great fable by Aesop. I had read the story when I was a little girl, but the lessons and revelations I gained from reading it as a forty-something adult was insightful. Two things struck me about the story:

The hare relied on what he always had for success (speed) – but never planned for what he would do without it. The tortoise had patience and consistency and was committed to his strengths. He knew he could not physically beat the hare, however he understood a breakthrough would come if he kept with his plan of being true to himself, through consistency to compete against the hare. The hare's pride did not make way for him to consider anything else, but speed to win, whilst the tortoise's observation of the hare highlighted his weak spot. The hare assumed speed would always bring him victory, but it became his downfall. He took it for granted. The tortoise won in the end.

A lot of people have a hare mentality. This is especially evident on social media. They got success from a viral moment, capitalised on it, and kept doing the same thing believing success is guaranteed. Then one day, they notice the success they had is gone and they have nothing to fall back on – as quickly as it came it went. They only did what was needed to maintain, doing things occasionally, because they took for granted the number of followers they have and that they would be interested in the same thing. They did not commit to consistency, because they did not have a goal or vision for other possible outcomes.

One evening as I was relaxing in the bath, God implored me to research two YouTubers that

I subscribe to: Daniel Ally and Terri Saville Foy, to find out how many videos got them to the success they have now. I was shocked to discover, that Terri Saville Foy, a motivational speaker and life coach, had created over seven hundred videos spanning fourteen years. Currently, she has 228,000 subscribers. Daniel Ally, has been on YouTube for six years and has 430,000 subscribers. The amount of time, dedication, and consistency they put in was evident. It was quite sobering when I compared the 150 videos that I created over three years, but it helped me to understand the truth about consistency being the essence of success. I realised that if I want my channel to be successful, I will need to be consistent, work hard and keep being creative.

However, consistency is difficult. It must be developed, and is a constant battle with what you can see. It means pushing past hard feelings and emotions when they scream at you to give up and quit. For instance, in the case of my YouTube channel, *Living the Empowered Life,* I must ignore the low view and subscriber count and continue the hard work of creating videos. Maybe for you, it is not seeing or feeling the weight drop off when you have been good on your diet and sticking to your eating plan. Or maybe it is doing an important job consistently and not getting recognition for it. Regardless of the circumstance, you must focus and train your mindset to embrace consistency, believing that if you commit to it, one day you *will* see success. One day, because you were slow and steady running with consistency you will win the race.

So I learned that I need to keep on and ignore the noise. I must ignore the subscriber count, the views, and the sometimes-present need for worldly validation of my efforts. I need to focus on what I do well and do it consistently, even though there are still times I am wobbly with it. In those moments I ask God for help, patience, and strength to run my race, because on my own I will probably give up. Because as God showed me slow and steady wins the race.

So why is consistency important?

It brings results.

It helps you to develop good habits and behaviours.

It helps you build endurance, longevity, inner resilience – and gives you staying power.

What are you trying to be consistent in? What is helping you to commit to it? I want to share with you my tips to build consistency:

Even if it's five minutes a day – commit to it

According to some scientific studies it takes anywhere from 18 days to 254 days for people to form a new habit (*Jamesclear.com*). If you spend a little time each day on your goal, every day consistently; sooner or later you will see results. It may take days, months, or even years – but keep at it.

Stop looking at what other people are doing

Looking at other people's journeys of success, when you are trying to be consistent in what you're struggling with will disappoint and discourage you. Focus on what *you* are doing.

Ask God for guidance

Ask God if the thing you are doing are what He wants you to do. It is slightly easier to be consistent in something when you know it is your God-given purpose. If He has put you on the path for what you are doing, if you ask God for help, He will help you be consistent with it.

I know it is hard, but do try and develop consistency in all that you do. It may not help you reach your goals quicker, but it will help you achieve them better. There is character building that only consistency can bring. Don't shortcut its journey.

And let us not grow weary while doing good, for in due season we shall reap if we do not lose heart. **Galatians 6.9**

Growth is the Ultimate Goal

Courage Does Not Include

I need to be real with you. If you are thinking about having the courage to make changes in your life, there are some things you need to know. First, do you know what courage is? According to the Oxford English Dictionary, it is: *'the ability to do something that frightens one; bravery'*. Furthermore, do you know there are different types of courage, such as physical, emotional, social, moral, and spiritual courage?

No matter what courage you are seeking to act upon, it doesn't include the perfect time or circumstances, a large amount of money sitting in a savings account, the agreement of family and friends, feeling it's 100% right, or knowing the exact outcome. Unfortunately, that is the way it is. That is why it is called courage. Otherwise, if it included these things, it would be called comfort.

In my book *Into the Unknown*, I recall in detail many situations in my life that required me to have courage. To have courage includes feeling scared, having doubts, not knowing how things will turn out, and taking risks. I know. It sounds uncomfortable, doesn't it? But that is how courage needs to be. It demands taking you into a place you've never known. A benefit I have learned about courage is that it is a great confidence builder. You discover new things about yourself and life. Everything I've achieved in my life so far, is down to having the courage to take risks. Oh, and of course having faith and praying to God. The bridge between where you are now in your life and where you desire to be; courage is the bridge you need to cross to get there.

You need courage because:

It will take you to the next level in your life.

It will build your confidence and increase your self-belief.

It will help you to seize new opportunities and experiences.

Courage means to act. I want to encourage you to take a courageous step towards the thing you want. Small steps lead to big action. For example, if you want to become a teacher, find out what qualifications you need or where you can start a course. Want to lose weight and need support? find out about where you can join a support group. Are you thinking about turning that hobby into a business? Why not set up a social media page and share your passion to gauge interest? Don't put off courage until tomorrow; seize the day today.

The Lord is my light and my salvation-whom shall, I fear? The Lord is the stronghold of my life- of whom should I be afraid? **Psalm 27:1**

Crab Bucket Mentality

So, I'm sure you have heard the saying 'show me your friends and I'll show you your future'. How about 'you are a reflection of the five closest people to you'? It is true. The people you keep around you will either help or hinder you. Hopefully, your friendships and relationships reflect love, positivity, support, trust, peace and promote and encourage a growth mindset in your life. As the bible scripture declares, iron sharpens iron (Proverbs 27:17). Your relationships should be both beneficial and reciprocal. Your relationships should not hold you back or wear you down. I have witnessed people stuck in relationships that keep them in a negative place. The people around them don't encourage them to progress, help them to change or encourage them to grow, because – if I'm being blunt – they are not bothered about bettering themselves.

I used to have people like this in my life, so I know what it›s like. For example, I had a friend many years ago – when I was a younger, less confident woman – who was quite happy for me to be the dysfunctional friend; the friend who always (unintentionally) messed up at times. She would make remarks in front of others about me and I would laugh it off, but her comments did upset me.

However, what that ex-friend didn›t know, was that I was working on myself (I didn›t share that with her, because I saw her negativity towards me) in private. She didn›t know that God was the power behind my change. When I started doing different things, she would try and tempt me to do the things I was trying to give up. She would offer her irrelevant opinions on why my new decisions weren›t going to work. But I was determined, and my decision led to positive changes in my life. Eventually, I broke away from the friendship.

I have heard soooo many stories from people who, when they decided to better themselves and change their lives, their friends, family, or partner turned against them. And naturally, of course, it is upsetting. The person blames their self for not seeing the signs, or for the response they have received. But you know, the signs would not be evident because it is not obvious when you are doing the same things, talking the same talk about 'I'm going to do this by next year', and lo and behold, next year comes and they're still doing the same things. They know the talk and accommodate it, because they see the pattern of the person. But it's that one day when something changes in that person, and they decide to change their life. That is when the crab bucket mentality shows itself. *God called each of us to be set apart and not conform to the ways of the world* (Romans 12:2). Jesus did not have a crab mentality and it is quite evident what happened to Jesus when he stood in truth and did what his father God called him to do. It caused his enemies to plot to crucify and kill him. People with a crab bucket mentality don't like people who go against the grain – they will sabotage you.

I have experienced people›s reactions to how I choose to live my life. When I decided not to move like everyone else around me (at the time) was doing, not conforming to cultural stereotypes and trauma patterns (not keeping in line with the trajectory of others from similar upbringing or experiences) people had a problem with me. I would get the 'you think you're better than' comments or treated differently, just because I chose to live my life unique to myself and follow God›s plan for me. Crab bucket mentality can even be seen in society, especially in the mass media and social media spheres. If most people don›t like a certain person and you like them, they have a problem with it. People will question your choice and give the same reason for not liking them, based on the opinion of thousands, if not millions of others. The crab bucket mentality is everywhere.

So what are the signs of crab bucket mentality relationships?

If you decide to have a different view, outlook, or opinion on something, they will treat you differently because of it.

People in your circle with crabs in a bucket will never openly celebrate your success because of their jealousy. Because your achievements highlight where they are stuck in life.

Crabs in a bucket (the people you hang around and are connected to) will drag you down, hold you back, and slow your progress. It will not matter to them what you are trying to do because they're not in a hurry to change, grow or do something different with their life.

Crabs in a bucket will not encourage you to do anything outside of what they are doing. So, if they are not doing it, why do you think they will encourage you to do it. They will keep you doing the same things because *they* are doing the same things.

The way to deal with people who have a crab bucket mentality, is to start to think and move independently from them. A crab bucket mentality puts you in a weak position, because it implies you cannot, or will not, think for yourself. It says you cannot move independently or that you are confident in being who God called you to be. It is also a sign that you need validation from others and is linked to possibly low self-esteem and confidence. If you recognise these signs among people in your life, or if you recognise that you operate with a crab-in-a-bucket mentality, what are you going to do to change it? If your desire to want to succeed, to live the life you want; if your desire to be exceptional is stronger than wanting to stick with relationships that keep you from discovering your potential, I encourage you to start to make moves of change. Don't keep yourself around people who feel insecure about you wanting to progress, or negative about you doing something different with your life. If they show the signs I have shared with you, is the negativity of their acquaintance enough to keep you from living the life you want?

The last thing you need if you are trying to soar like an eagle to new heights in your life, is to be weighed down by people with a crab bucket mentality. It is okay to live your own life and be your own person. Give yourself permission.

Do not be deceived: Evil company corrupts good habits. **1 Corinthians 15:33**

Define Your Personal Success

Society, namely social media, and the media in general, try and define people's perception of success. You only need to scroll through Instagram to see what I mean. For example, the accounts of self-professed 'entrepreneurs', show endless holidays, pictures of flash cars, and shopping at designer stores, yet you will never see them at a desk working or showing a visual real-life representation of a day in the life of their business. These images and messages that we are constantly bombarded with are enough to make the average confident person think that what they are doing is not enough; or that they are enough. That is why plastic surgery is more popular than ever; millions of people are just not happy with themselves – or their accomplishments.

Success should mean different things to different people, but instead, society has encouraged it to be measured by the acquirement of material goods, money and looks. It does not take into consideration the individual person's drive, motivation, abilities, or desired outcomes. That is why it is important to have your own definition of personal success. I know this can be hard to define. I suffered from depression for two decades, but it helped me to define my personal success because most days were challenging. Every day I had to set myself small tasks and completing them gave me a feeling of accomplishment. Applying this method, helped me to define my idea of personal success even further. If you struggle with the world's idea of success and want to develop your own personalised individual version, I want to share with you three tips to help you:

Complete what you set out to do

Whatever your goal is, see it through to the end. There is no harm in starting with a small goal and working your way towards bigger goals. It is not the size of the task that matters – only that you complete it.

Don't compare your life with other people's

Where you are in life right now is where you need to be. You can work on enhancing it so that you can live the best life you can. Life is not a competition. Start to appreciate your uniqueness and celebrate the life God has given you.

Overcome challenges

As I mentioned; personal success can be found in overcoming mistakes, depression, trauma, anxiety, and many other challenges. When you can overcome those things in your life that once seemed undefeatable – that is a huge accomplishment. It is also personal encouragement to continue in other areas of your life to define success. Work on one issue at a time and be patient with yourself.

Do not let anyone define to you what success is in your life. Define your own success, create your own path and be happy with what you achieve. It may not mean anything to other people, but what matters is that it means something to you.

Commit your works to the Lord, and your thoughts will be established. **Proverbs 16:3**

Empowered Life Killers

So many people are not living empowered. They are living afraid, stuck, bored, repetitive, courage-less, boxed in, and stressed out. I am sure that you get my drift; does this sound like someone living an empowered life?

My question to you is: are you living an empowered life? If the answer is yes, then more life to you! However, if the answer is no, what is stopping you? The truth is you are stopping yourself. Why do I believe that? Because regardless of the situation that you find yourself in, you can still find a way to empower yourself. Stuck in a horrible job? You can work on getting the job you want! You are not tied to the job. No one is forcing you to stay there. Not even debt is forcing you to stay there, because you can still look for a job that you do not dread going to and that does not make you negative, cry or feel depressed. If you are in a relationship stuck between a rock and a hard place, meaning, you don›t want to leave the person, but they won›t change, well, work on you, and do things that you enjoy. Do not tie your happiness to other people. Living an empowered life is living your life despite circumstances and situations outside of your control.

At the moment I am studying for a master's degree. One of the factors I have discovered that is important for entrepreneurs – to get through the uncertain and difficult journey of entrepreneurship – is locus control. Locus control is the extent to which the entrepreneur believes they have control over situations in their life, and how they learned to live with it whilst pursuing opportunities. I believe locus control is not just important for the entrepreneur, but for every person who desires to live an empowered life. You must take control of your decisions; you cannot allow outside factors to determine what you do. Living an Empowered Life is also about accessing power and self-authority in the precise moments you feel you do not have it. So, what kills living an empowered life?

Living your life for other people

Are you living your life on the recommendations, influence, and advice of other people? Are you doing things because they, meaning friends, family, and parents want you to do it? I'm sorry to say – well I am not sorry to say, because I am telling you the truth – you are not living an empowered life, you are living your life for other people. How can you live an empowered life, which is basically living a life authentic to you, when you are living it for someone else? I know it probably sounds harsh, but if this is you, you have got to find a way to live your life for yourself. You must first develop the confidence to believe that you can be trusted with decisions concerning your life. Even if you make mistakes, it's okay; do not give your power away.

Comfort

We have touched on this subject a few times throughout this book. If you want to stay in the familiar, you cannot progress to live exceptional and not expected. Comfortable, repetitive, and familiar is nice, but if you want to live an empowered life, the two cannot work together. Think about it. Think about the things you have wanted to do for such a long time. Ask yourself why haven't you done it? If you are being honest, comfort is the reason why. Comfort in the same thing. Comfort in living in fear – yes, comfort with the fear of not taking a step towards the things you want to do is a form of comfort! The bottom line is, if you want to change your life, do new or different things, or follow your dreams – you cannot do it in your comfort zone.

Not open to ideas, opportunities, or new ways of doing things

If you are not open to life, you will not live an empowered life. It is not hard to be open to possibilities, but it is hard if you are set in your ways, because your ways will have to change to have openness. Your comfort ways, your mindset ways (meaning what you are used to seeing, thinking, doing ways). You can be open to new ideas, opportunities, or new ways to do things and lack confidence or low self-esteem at the same time. These are action issues rather than mindset issues. If you want to act on your openness, I have resources such as the courage course and empowerment coaching services to support you to act. Life living you, rather than you living life, is not living. You can change it, because you hold the power to change it – do not let anyone tell you differently.

Empowered life killers can be stopped by learning to be flexible about life, true to yourself, exposing yourself to risk (new experiences, etc) making different choices, and changing your behaviour, mindset, and actions. The key is to keep moving, adapt, and live your life authentically. You don't want to remain the same, stay stuck or be stagnant– flow with the rhythm of life.

I called on the Lord in distress; The Lord answered me and set me in a broad place. **Psalm 118:5**

Exceptional Not Expected

To be exceptional is an important part of Living the Empowered Life. You will find it is one of the things that sets someone apart from those around them, because they are doing high-quality things that others are not doing.

I believe that everyone should aspire to be exceptional in life. Even in the times I struggled with depression, if it was one thing that I could do, I would do it well and to a high standard. It is my hallmark; you won›t find me putting myself, my name, or my business endeavours into anything that is done mediocre, or half-hearted.

It is a different level from expected to exceptional. To be exceptional requires you to push past inner and outer boundaries. To be expected, is to stay within the confines of what you've always been doing, and remain at the same level in life. You never push beyond your level of understanding and limitations. To stay at the expected level, invites disappointment, because you never stretch to break out; you hold back. It's about not being challenged to discover yourself. And do you know what? I believe you should always have an element of surprise about yourself. Even surprising yourself about… yourself! I believe no one should see you coming (be able to predict your actions, decisions, choices, or outcomes of what you can do).

'Be Exceptional not Expected' is what I tell my sixteen-year-old daughter all the time, (I say this, especially about how she carries herself, her school grades, and encouraging her to explore her potential and to do more than what is required of her). I tell her to always aim to be exceptional, not to let her teachers believe they know exactly what she is capable of. And the same pep talk I give to her is the same I am giving to you. Don›t let those around you – your family, friends, colleagues and even your self-limiting thoughts – dictate what you are capable of. Don›t allow others to limit you with their expectations.

So, what is the difference between being exceptional and expected?

To be 'expected', means people have a pre-conceived notion of what they believe is the most you can do. To be 'exceptional', means you *exceed* their expectations and estimation, cast off your own constraints and push yourself to achieve excellence in all that you do. You may be thinking, why should being exceptional and not expected matter? Because it's about striving for personal growth – to be the best you can be.

So how do you know you are exceptional not expected? Some indicators are:

People cannot second guess you and are surprised when you do something they didn't expect.

You aim to be more than average.

You exceed in everything you set out to do.

You have goals that you are actively seeking to fulfil.

You have high standards for yourself and your life, and desire quality in every area.

You exceed other people's estimations of you and your abilities.

You do more than is required of you, not because of people, but because you have high standards.

I consistently do all of these things. Why? Because I understood from a young age, coming from a dysfunctional and disadvantaged background, that hard work, doing things outside the box, going the extra mile, and carrying myself with integrity and high standards would set me apart. It took years to cultivate the mindset and attitude to be the woman I am now. It is ingrained in my character; it is my trademark – my personal standard.

Everyone can be Expected, but few can be Exceptional. Why? Because many people do not want to put in the hard work, effort and sacrifice it takes to reach that level.

If you want to take your life up a level from Expected to Exceptional

Be diligent.

Find something that sets you apart from others and develop and master it.

Set standards for your life, work, and you as a person.

Consistently set new challenges for yourself and stretch outside of your comfort zone.

Set yourself the challenge to up your game, and up your levels in life. Decide on one thing you are going to do to push beyond your limitations in that area.

Don't do just enough to get by in life. Be the type of person who likes to do things well, more than expected and to a high standard. Aim to live your life to its fullest by taking every opportunity to be the best you can be.

Then this Daniel distinguished himself above the governors and satraps because an excellent spirit was in him, and the king gave thought to set him over the whole realm. **Daniel 6:3**

Four Negative Cs

To be exceptional and not expected, requires you to avoid attitudes, behaviours, and habits that will hold you back from living to your full potential. I talk to you about the four Cs and why you should avoid them. These four Cs are depressing, debilitating and anti-everything that living an empowered life is about. I believe we have all indulged in their offerings at some point in life. However, to indulge is different than to live with and accept. So, these are the four Cs to avoid:

Complaining is a sign of ungratefulness. Complaining takes the power to change things out of your hands and gives whatever the situation is power over you. Complaining indicates discontentment. In another context, complaining about poor customer service can be a positive thing to do. However, we are talking about complaining in the context of living an empowered life and complaining is not something that will help you live it. I would encourage you, rather than complain, to think about how you can change the situation, or use it to empower yourself.

Compromise is the enemy of self. Compromise causes confusion, because nothing is clear. Compromising indicates you are not completely on your own side. Why half-step with yourself? Here are a few reasons why people short-change themselves by compromising: people pleasing, wanting acceptance and validation from others, low confidence and/or self-esteem issues, and not being clear about where they stand in life. Compromising is straddling the fence. God talks about those who compromise as being lukewarm (Romans 3:16). In particular it refers to those who profess to be Christian, who have given their life to Christ, yet still engage in a life of known sin. In this way, compromise is living in an unauthentic and undecided way. You cannot be 50/50 with yourself and expect great outcomes. You need to decide whether to give yourself and the things that you want to do, one hundred per cent commitment, or don't do them at all. You can't push and pull at the same time. If you struggle with compromise, I suggest taking time to think about what you really want. There should be non-negotiables and standards when it comes to you, regardless of outside influences and circumstances.

Complacency is dangerous. Have your past successes caused you to take your foot off the gas? Have you cut corners, taken shortcuts, not put the same effort in, or given your all to the things you want to achieve, because you think you›ve arrived? Beware: complacency is in your midst. Regardless of whether or not you have reached your goal, consistent energy is needed throughout life. One thing I've heard very successful entrepreneurs say; even when you achieve success you never arrive. There is always work to be done to improve, develop, to discover. To be exceptional and not expected in life requires, the same effort. Don't rest on your laurels. To maintain where you are, to accomplish more – complacency must go.

Comparing, is robbing yourself of the chance to develop into uniquely who you are supposed to be. A while back on Instagram, I wrote: to compare is to impair. Never compare yourself to others; it will diminish you. Because that is what you are doing with comparison. As I mentioned in my earlier point about compromise, it only short-changes you.

So, if you have any of these four Cs in your life, start to think of ways to turn them into positives. Deal with unresolved issues, try new experiences, engage in positivity, take courage, and make decisions that empower you. Do not feel bad or guilty about any struggles you have had with any of the four Cs, as it changes nothing. Focus on the good news that they can be changed – and you have the power to change them.

In everything give thanks; for this is the will of God in Christ Jesus for you. **1 Thessalonians 5:18**

Four Positive Cs

The positive 4 Cs are things that will enrich your life and change it for the better.

Courage...

Is the driving force behind living an empowered life. Courage opens doors. Courage helps you to explore life. Courage breeds opportunities. And courage flies in the face of fear, helps you to take risks, and helps you to go after your goals and dreams. If you don't know how to have courage, start by trying new things.

Consistency...

Is hard to maintain at times, especially when you cannot see any reward for your efforts. However, sooner or later, consistency will pay off. For example, I experienced this with my first book *Daughter Arise*. I launched it in 2010 and sales were great in the beginning. Then sales slowed down to five sales a month. Although, my book experienced a resurgence five years ago, resulting in multiple sales every month. The point is; my book is twelve years old. I could have given up on my book years ago, but I remained consistent in talking about it, posting it on social media and reminding people about its message. I kept chipping away at it because I believed in it. And I believe consistency helps passion, belief, vision and to keep in focus the 'WHY' factor when things are challenging.

Change…

You know the saying – it's as good as a rest. Change is the variety of life. It keeps you on your toes. It is the key to personal and self-development. It sharpens the senses and is the medicine for complacency. I have gone out of my way over the past six years, to change a lot of things about my life and it has been influenced and linked to my goals, which have helped me to live an intentional life. God has been the one in the driving seat and guided and helped me to change (psalm 32.8). The main thing you need to know about change, is that it is good for the mind, body, and soul. When was the last time you had a change? A change of life direction, or a change of routine? Look at making small changes first, and the bigger changes you want to make won't seem so daunting.

Compassion…

Do you show compassion to others? Kindness to others? Well, show compassion to you. Be kind to yourself when you don't meet your goals, and congratulate yourself for the fact you tried. How do you deal with the things you don't like about yourself? Do you criticise or belittle yourself? How about showing yourself grace, warmth, and love? You see, without self-compassion, the alternative is self-judgement. Self-judgement will kill your attempts to naturally grow from expected to exceptional. It is much better to be nice to yourself. You can be mindful of where you are on your journey, acknowledging that things might not be where you'd hoped they are, but not dwelling and beating yourself up about it. When you make that choice, you allow room for self-compassion to do its kind work. So, give yourself a break today, get off your own back and be compassionate to yourself.

This is the day the Lord has made; We will rejoice and be glad in it. **Psalm 118:24**

Get Out of Your Own Way

Have you ever wanted to do something new or different, but are hesitant? Do you come up with more excuses and reasons why you should not do that thing rather than just going for it? Or personally, do you find reasons not to like, love or accept yourself? If this is you, you need to get out of your own way! Because you are the biggest block in reaching your potential!

People get in their own way for many reasons, such as:

They feel they do not deserve better.

Lack of confidence.

Used to viewing self in a negative light.

They do not feel the thing they desire to change, accomplish, or pursue is obtainable.

I used to get in my own way because I didn't think I was worthy of anything good. I got out of my own way, by undertaking therapy. Healing from things that led me to believe I was not worthy, helped me to view myself, my capabilities, and my potential in a different light. Also, I made peace with myself, embraced myself, and explored opportunities. The main thing I learned about getting out of my own way was I had to give myself permission to be! Give yourself permission to want better, to be yourself, to be the person you want to be, and to pursue the things you want in life.

If you want to get out of your own way you can:

Give things a try at least once. Do not let fear stop you

Do not listen to negative self-talk.

Give yourself permission to do new things.

Do not put limits on yourself.

Be open to new possibilities.

Work on building your confidence and self-esteem.

Embrace who you are and work with it.

Replace negative self-talk replace it with positive affirmation.

Getting in your own way is a form of self-sabotage. Do not block yourself. There are enough challenges in life without you adding to them.

Ask, and it will be given to you; seek, and you will find; knock, and it will be opened to you. 8 For everyone who asks receives, and he who seeks finds, and to him who knocks it will be opened. **Matthew 7:7-11**

Have You Allowed Life to Get the Better of You?

I have witnessed so many people, especially women, allow life to get the better of them. Their life, relationships, job, finances, and people have grinded them into the ground. It is really upsetting to see people trapped in their own life. Hope is gone, they are resigned to accept whatever comes their way; feeling that no options or choices are available to them. Is that you? Have you allowed life to get the better of you?

I understand. It is a painful place to be in. I know, because I have been there. In the past I allowed life to get the better of me; finances, circumstances, and people – but as if these things weren't bad enough, I berated myself on top of it, because when I saw that life was getting the better of me, I gave myself a hard time. Rather than looking at things I could change, I would say things like 'I›m useless', 'why can›t you just do...' It was psychologically debilitating to engage in this mental beatdown. I was seemingly beaten by life on the outside and feeling defeated, without hope on the inside; yet something still refused to let me give in. Getting through each day was a blessing. And to be honest, I would not have gotten through it without the strength of the Living God. Eventually, after going through a repeated negative cycle of allowing life to get the better of me, a desire to break free, and a desire to want to live a better life superseded those feelings of not trying and giving in.

It can be a culmination of things, or one situation, circumstance or event, that serves as an open door, that allows life to get the better of you. Lack of vision, motivation, not engaging in fulfilling and meaningful pursuits, not having goals in life, just doing enough to get by – and basically not stewarding your own life – are some of the reasons that it happens. Allowing life to get the better of you, manifests itself in the following ways: emotional/binge eating, lethargy, lack of self-control and discipline, low self-esteem and confidence, lack of drive or ambition, lack of enthusiasm, negativity, and depression.

You see, until you realise and understand that you have choices in your own life, and that *you* have the power to change it, set boundaries and define it, life will continue to get the better of you. You will continue to stay trapped or upset. *You must take back control.* It will mean making changes. It will mean stepping out of your comfort zone. It may involve upsetting people around you, who for far too long have been taking liberties and been used to you giving in. They won't like the changes, but it is not about them – it is about you. I had to battle to get ownership of my own life and I had to stop allowing it to defeat me. It took years of practice; building my self-esteem and developing confidence through new experiences; facing and overcoming difficulties to get a hold of my life. I can't promise you that any situation you have allowed to get the better of you (I say 'allowed' because no one has forced you to put up with it) will not upset you, make you uncomfortable or not require a sacrifice, but you have the choice to remain or breakthrough whatever is holding you back in life. Ask yourself this question: do you believe this is what you deserve? Do you desire change? You own your life and are in control of the decisions you make regarding it. It starts with your desire to want more out of life. Here are three tips to help you reclaim your life and not allow it to get the better of you:

Appreciate the good in yourself

Embrace positively your traits, your skills, your strengths – and even your weakness. Learn to love yourself in the here and now, not in the person you want to become in the future. Self-rejection is the worst thing you can do to yourself. Self-appreciation, whilst knowing you are not perfect, or even where you want to be life, will do you a lot of good.

Invest in self-care

Do things that build your self-esteem and confidence. Engage in activities that make you feel good about yourself. Self-care is important to the mind, body, soul, and spirit. Do things that nourish you inwardly and on the outside.

Pick a battle

Pick one thing you want to have personal victory in (hint: start with something small and something you can have control over) and write down some ideas of things that will help you to deal with it.

Connect with something that brings you joy

When you lose hope in your life it can affect everything. No enthusiasm, inspiration or motivation leads to anxiety, depression and giving up. I encourage you to reconnect with something that brings you joy. The thing that puts a smile on your face, that thing you forgot a long time ago. You see, that is where you can start to reclaim your life.

Hope deferred makes the heart sick, but when the desire comes, it is a tree of life. **Proverbs 13:12**

How To Be Comfortable in Your Own Skin

For the longest time, I was not comfortable in my own skin. One of the main things I remember during that long and painful period in my life, which was a direct effect of the childhood sexual abuse I endured, is feeling that I was not enough, not good enough. Not being comfortable in my own skin meant that I spent money focusing on my outside appearance. I spent too much time on self-assessment (focusing on all the things I felt were wrong with me, instead of self-acceptance (focusing on being at peace with myself). I felt there was an invisible bar that I could never reach.

I discovered, that even though I was able to heal from past hurts and trauma, I realised I was still broken inside. Not accepting myself and focusing on my external appearance and other things, were symptoms of my brokenness and not being comfortable in my own skin – and life. One of the major catalysts in my starting to be comfortable in my own skin, was the desire to be at peace with myself. I remember turning forty years old, as the point when I started to embrace everything that was me. Maybe it was a natural progression with age. Whatever the catalyst was, I welcomed it. Now I need to say that a major part of being comfortable in my own skin, came from accepting who I was, despite my inner challenges and not from validation based on my appearance or external achievements. And ever since, I have been working at being comfortable in my own skin every day, loving and accepting myself through prayer, self-care and being kind to myself.

Being comfortable in your skin is a big part of being exceptional and not expected, and in you living an empowered life. It is a major influence key in having courage, taking risks, and doing things that those around us are not doing. It is essential to your personal growth. It helps you to be yourself wherever you are.

To be comfortable in your own skin you must:

Embrace and accept yourself (the good, the bad, the ugly).

Kill people-pleasing.

Learn to be happy in your own company (be as comfortable around people as you are by yourself).

Be confident in who you are no matter the situation (happy to be in your own lane).

Not compare yourself to others (remember: to compare is to impair).

No matter how you feel about yourself, whether you feel you measure up to your standards or other people's standards, God loves you. Get comfortable being you and accept yourself as you are – not who you want to be. That will come in time. Once you can do that, your journey to where you want to be in life will be much easier.

*For I am persuaded that neither death nor life, nor angels nor principalities nor powers, nor things present nor things to come, **39** nor height nor depth, nor any other created thing, shall be able to separate us from the love of God which is in Christ Jesus our Lord. Whether you are comfortable in your skin or not nothing can separate us from his love for us.* **Romans 8 38-39**

How to Develop Courage

Just the mention of the word 'courage', is enough to create fear in people's hearts and minds. The word is synonymous with doing big, bold, and scary things; doing things that may be out of character with what people expect of you. To have courage can seem impossible. Do you think or believe this about having courage?

Yes, it is true. Courage does require action. However, the process of having courage does not have to be overwhelming. Rather than looking at courage as an insurmountable mountain, how about taking it one step at a time? It is easier said than done I know. Especially when you don't know what steps to take or even what those steps will entail. Having said that, having a *plan* makes the goal or task easier. I found that helped me on my own courageous journey to do different things. That is why I created The Courage Course, an online course to help people take courageous action to go after their goals and dreams. Besides helping people to understand the process of courage, it also supports them to develop an action plan and provides encouragement and empowerment every step of the way. No longer will someone – who wants to develop courage – have to remain stuck, or wonder how they will get from where they are now, to where they want to be. Because goals and dreams are attainable and achievable, with access to a resource that will facilitate progressive action. Developing courage can also be found in doing small things such as:

Saying 'no' when you always say 'yes'

Low self-esteem, intimidation by someone, other circumstances or just not putting your needs first, are factors that can play a part in always saying 'yes'. You can start to find the courage by saying 'no' to things you do not want to do. After a while, you will find that because you developed the courage to say no to small things, over time it will be easier to say no to bigger decisions.

Making new or different decisions

Are you always doing the same things? Comfortable because you never change your situation or make new decisions? This is the perfect opportunity to develop your courage muscle! Say yes to something new – give it a try and see what happens.

Do one thing a day towards your goal, dream, or life change that you want

This is where having a plan comes in handy, because you can plan the steps. What is it that you want to do? Today do one thing towards achieving it. This is your opportunity to take courageous action. Go for it and seize the day!

But you, take courage! Do not let your hands be weak, for your work shall be rewarded. **2 Chronicles 15**

Fear Requires You
Live in Conformity
Courage Frees
You to Live
Authentically

How to Find Inspiration

Life at times can be boring, repetitive, and mundane. It's in these times, that life needs some zhuzhing up (not sure that's an actual word but you know what I mean; something a little different). And I think I have found the answer to make it exciting: inspiration.

So, what is so special about inspiration? Well... inspiration is free and can be found anywhere at any time. The imagination powers inspiration. It allows you to explore possibilities freely without physical constraints, without the can and can›t dos of the realities of life. It can be hard to act upon inspiration when it feels life has hemmed you in. However, it is in those moments when you feel trapped, that inspiration is needed more than ever; it's that place that allows you to escape into the thing you love. When I reflect on my four-year journey of stepping into the unknown to become an entrepreneur, it feels surreal that I am here living and doing it. I spent years doing jobs that I was not passionate about, but the thing that kept me going in those challenging years were inspiration and creativity. Even now, when I have seasons of hardship and challenges – because life (at times) has been kicking my you know what – I don›t know where I would be without these two outlets; not just in my ventures, but in life in general.

Inspiration has given me hope and got me through some difficult and dark times.

So let me tell you *why* I love inspiration so much.

It allows me to dream big.

It makes me feel hopeful.

It is the fertile soil from where my ideas are birthed.

It allows me to be creative.

It empowers me.

If, at the moment in your life, you find yourself in a dry, stagnant place – bored, uninspired and lacking motivation. Not enthusiastic about the present or future, then may I suggest that you need a dose of inspiration. You need to think about things that *excite* you, and that bring you a sense of joy. Things that stir something inside of you, to want to do something new, go in a different direction and breathe new life into your soul. Things that get your mind off your challenges. What is that thing? What inspires you? When was the last time you were inspired and what did that result in?

Inspiration can be found anywhere. It could be a book that you have read, or a person that has influenced you in a positive way. A love for something that is dear to you. If you are not sure how to get your inspiration flowing again, you can try the following tips:

Create a vision board

I created a vision board five years ago and I upgraded it to make a bigger one. I made a bigger version, because I was continually inspired by so many things that fuelled new dreams. Vision boards are inspiring as they give you a visual image of the things you want to do. All you need is a piece of card, scissors, glue and old magazines/newspapers and you're good to go.

Get out and about

Go to your favourite places for inspiration or visit somewhere fun or new, or somewhere you've always loved to visit. I love going to art exhibitions, book fairs, and jazz club dinners. I find these activities inspiring, sophisticated and different. They always give me ideas for creative content and inspiration. Find somewhere to go that introduces you to a different side of life. What better way to find inspiration than engaging in things that give you a sense of joy or happiness? Trust me, if you do this, inspiration won't be hard to find.

Draw inspiration from others

On my YouTube channel *Living the Empowered Life* I have created videos on people who inspire me: Jackie Pullinger, Karl Lagerfeld, Folorunsho Alakjia, Maya Angelou, and Ben Carson to name but a few. With each person, I have found something inspiring about them; how they work, their character, how they've dealt with difficulties, and how they lead and empower others. It's not idol worship to feel inspired by others (that is where you have made the person your God, or you want to be them, live their life, dress, walk and talk like them). People are not perfect, but you can find something in their story, life or experiences that inspire you, help you have courage, develop, or motivate you on your life journey.

Write down your ideas

I have notebooks upon notebooks of ideas, boxes of post-its, and over 600 notes on both of my phones. Ideas, and acting upon them in due season, are my thing. That's why I'm doing a master's degree in innovation management and entrepreneurship. Ideas are from the imagination, and they are the greatest gift God has given me. God is my greatest source of inspiration. Through His Holy Spirit, God fed my mind with inspirational knowledge, which allowed me to believe I can do and be the person I wanted to be. Write down your ideas, those thoughts that are 'A-ha!' moments, those 'I would love to'… Sometimes people say to themselves 'I don't get inspired', but it's just they forget about moments like these. If you write them down, you can always go back to them. You will be surprised at how inspired thoughts can play a part in something you want to do later down the line.

And the last thing I want to tell you that will help release inspiration in your life, is to change the way you view yourself – and your capabilities. Allow yourself to *be*. You can be inspired despite what is going on in your life, or how you may feel about the life you are living now. Your mind is not trapped unless you allow it to be. If you allow yourself to be inspired down the road, it will be the motivation fuel you need to make positive life changes. It was for me. Inspiration can lead you on an exciting journey if you allow it. It will give you the courage to explore your dreams; give you hope for your future and allow you to do more than you imagine. Tap into inspiration and let it become part of your everyday life.

Now to him who is able to do exceedingly abundantly above all that we ask or think, according to the power that works in us. **Ephesians 3:20**

How to Have Peace in Troubled Times

2020 was a perfect example of a troubling year. The pandemic, sudden deaths, financial hardship, and loss of jobs were some of the challenging circumstances many people faced. At one point I thought my business would not survive this tumultuous time. It's not hard to see why there was a spike in mental health issues, anxiety, depression, and suicide. I realised during that time more than ever, that I needed to take better care of my mental health. I learned that when I started to do things to look after it, I felt an inner calm and had a tremendous sense of peace.

One of the biggest threats to my peace was wanting to know the outcome of situations outside of my control. It was like I was fighting against the waves of life only to be pushed back. The more I pushed the more frustrated I got. Focusing on the very things that were unsolvable at the time, caused me more harm than good. I had to change what I was doing, I decided to let go and let God take care of it (Jeremiah 29:11).

It did not happen overnight, but in cultivating habits, setting boundaries, and not putting stress on myself, little changes started to happen. Now that I am out of that turbulent season, those changes continue to benefit my life. Even though I still face challenges, I know how to hold on and have peace in troubling times. If you are experiencing a lack of inner peace or facing mental health issues, I want to share with you some tips that helped me:

Pray

God is an ever-present help in times of trouble (Psalm 46:1) – I have found that to be true in my darkest times. Turn to Living God and through His Son Jesus Christ, he will give you peace. Spend time in his presence. Read the bible and pray. I know it doesn't seem exciting, but it is in the unassuming things that value is found. If you don't know how to talk to God, I have left a little prayer for you in the back of this book.

Limit screen time

Watching and reading the news constantly because you worry about what in the world is going on is not good for the mind. Scrolling endlessly through social media, filling your mind with all kinds of unwanted messages can affect the mind greatly. Try and limit these habits; instead, why not read a book or do things that you enjoy that don't involve the screen?

Focus on the positive

It is very easy to look at all that is wrong in the world. However, I found peace in focusing on the positive and giving thanks to God for the blessings that I had. Each day, try and find at least one positive to hold on to. Be thankful, for there is always someone out there that has worse circumstances – not to take away from what you may be going through, though it does help to give a sense of perspective.

Have quiet time

People underestimate the power of quiet time. It is one of the main things that really helped my mental health. Just to sit still and do nothing. Sometimes I just go and sit in the park by the lake. No music, no noise just quiet. It really is rewarding. Even if it is once a week; schedule quiet time for you. You could start with an hour and build up to as much time as you want. You will be surprised at how it replenishes the mind and soul.

Accept the things you can't change and accept where you are. It is okay to have expectations, but it may not happen in the time you expected it. You must go with the flow. In doing so, you relieve pressure off yourself and in turn, you will relieve your mind and experience peace.

Peace, I leave with you, my peace I give to you; not as the world gives do I give to you. Let not your heart be troubled, neither let it be afraid **(John 14:27)**

In the Waiting

Are you are waiting for something to happen? Maybe you have created a product and you are waiting for sales. Or maybe you are waiting for that job to come up that you have had your eye on for ages, for things to change in a difficult situation, or waiting for a breakthrough in personal challenges. You have put in the effort, time, work, and prayer – but nothing. What do you do when there is no breakthrough, result or answer?

The place of waiting is extremely difficult. It requires patience, wisdom, and discernment (because sometimes, the place of waiting can give the appearance that nothing is happening and trick you out of position). The place of waiting is unknown, because you don't know if you are going to wait an hour, a day, a week, months, years, or even decades! Here is a list of some things I have waited for, for a long time for: Thirty-two years waiting for justice for the sexual abuse I experienced as a child. Fourteen years for proper reconciliation with my estranged first daughter. Four years (so far) for a continuous stream of income and contracts for my business. What I noticed in all these different situations of waiting for a breakthrough, is that none of them are in my control, because they are dependent on people, circumstances, the right time, and opportunities. So, how did I manage the waiting? There were three things that I noticed in how I handled it:

Patience

Not good at first. I was never a patient person, but waiting humbled me. Everything is outside of my control: what can I do? I had to ask God for help with the patience to wait. Also, trust God's timing because he knows best. I may not like having to wait, but that is just the way it is.

Attitude

At first, I had a bad attitude in waiting. I had already been through enough. I wanted things to happen *now* and couldn't understand why it was not happening. I felt entitled, yet I knew I was entitled to nothing; pride and a bad attitude result in delay.

Blame

Waiting also made me believe that I must have done something wrong, because the things I desired had not come to pass yet. I centred the reason around me, instead of thinking from a broader perspective.
The key thing that I've done in the waiting, is work on myself. I became empowered in my situations and challenges by understanding that I held the power to change only ME. Through prayer, and changing

my perspective on everything, allowed the process of patience to develop, using the time of 'waiting' to my advantage, rather than focusing on things I can do nothing about has helped me to be at peace with whatever outcome that happens. So here are three things to be aware of and use to prepare yourself while you wait:

Your attitude

Be mindful of how waiting defines you.

Preparation

What you do in the waiting period will prepare you for what you are waiting for.

Reflection

What have you learned in the waiting? In the quiet moments. Have you grown, developed as a person, and identified areas within you that you need to work on? Do you see situations differently, or the same?

I want to leave you with this: be happy in the waiting, be present in waiting, meaning that you engage in the lessons, ups and downs and experiences that may happen in the waiting. Don't resent it. Don't ignore the blessings it can bring. Everything happens for a reason.

To everything, there is a season, A time for every purpose under heaven. **Ecclesiastes 3:1**

Ingredients to Living an Empowered Life

What does it mean to be empowered? It is a process that fosters power. It helps you gain control over your life. Living an empowered life is made up of a mixture of things. I want to share with you the ingredients. These are things based on my own experience. These things have helped me along my life journey to live exceptional and not expected:

Taking risks.

Dealing with unresolved trauma, issues, and healing.

Acting on ideas.

Making intentional choices.

Gaining more knowledge.

Building my self-esteem and confidence.

Having courage.

Actively looking for positive solutions to problems.

Building positive relationships.

Investing time in personal development.

Develop a relationship with God through Jesus Christ.

Finding purpose and living it.

Not settling for less.

Living my life unique to me.

There are a couple of things that I need you to know about the recipe. I found the first ingredient in my early twenties (I am in my mid-forties now, at the time of writing). I didn't get all the ingredients in one go. To make good use of all the ingredients, I had to adapt, adjust, and apply each ingredient with action. It involved therapy. I had lots of it. It involved building my self-esteem and confidence. Facing fears and stepping out of my comfort zone not just physically but mentally. It involved doing new and different things, learning from mistakes, self-love and knowing my worth in the eyes of God. And just like the ingredients of a recipe, I adjusted things to get it right.

God, through His Holy Spirit, equipped and helped me to live an empowered life. But I had to take the action. It is a process of learning, exploring, and taking action to live it. It does not happen overnight and cannot be rushed.

Are there things you already know but you have not acted on? What are your ingredients? (Similar to having ingredients in the cupboard that you forgot you had!) think about how you can start to use them. Nobody's recipe is the same. The key is to find out how much you need in good measure to live an empowered, fulfilling life.

I am the vine; you are the branches. He who abides in me, and I in him, bears much fruit; for without me you can do nothing. **John 15:5**

Journal Your Journey

Since the age of twenty-one years old (I am forty-six now!) I have constantly kept a journal. My journal journey started whilst I was recovering in a mental health clinic after suffering a nervous breakdown. It was a foster carer – who I had from the age of sixteen to eighteen years old– who on a visit to see me, popped into the Waterstones bookstore across the road from the clinic. At night, when I was left alone with my thoughts, I wrote down my feelings. Being able to express *me* on paper, was natural to me. I had written many poems and other expressive content over the years, and to be able to express my thoughts, hopes, dreams and fears, without feeling that I would be condemned for it, helped me to start my healing journey from the many painful things that I experienced.

Over the years I have amassed a large collection of completed journals. I do not tend to look at them often, but when I do, I am amazed and grateful for how far the Lord God has brought me. Looking at the different entries from the different eras of my life reminds me of my strength, growth and personal growth and development. Moreover, it feels like I am reading about someone else when I revisit the different chapters of my life. If you have not journaled before, I want to encourage you to give it a try. There are many benefits:

It helps you to express yourself.

It is the ultimate self-development tool – it helps you to monitor your highs and lows, and you can capture your successes and reflect on your mistakes.

It is self-empowerment – you don't need permission from others to do it.

It helps you to emotionally process your day and clear your mind.

You don't need a fancy notebook to start –any A5 size notebook will do. You can start with one entry a week and progress until you get into the rhythm of journaling consistently. To live exceptional and not expected, does require some form of monitoring of your life progression so that you can feel encouraged by any changes that you notice about yourself in life. Journaling is a great way to do it – so give it a try.

Your word is a lamp to my feet and a light to my path.
Psalm 119:105

Passion and Purpose Wins

I am really inspired by the work of Mr Brainwash (Thierry Guetta), a contemporary French artist based in L.A. I have been a fan of his work for a while now. Recently, I got to view his work at a fine art gallery; it was inspiring. Mr Brainwash uses the quote 'follow your dreams', to inspire those who look at his pop and street art paintings. As I stood amazed at his beautiful art, I began to wonder how he followed his dream.

I found out that he didn't start off as an artist. In fact, he was an amateur videographer and proprietor of a second-hand clothes store. His cousin Invader (a street artist) introduced him to art. Fast forward a decade later – his life is on a different trajectory. His paintings command six figures. His murals are seen all over the world. He is commissioned by celebrities to design album covers and artwork. Mr Brainwash is living a dream because he discovered a passion for painting. It became his life's work. He has claimed this dream as his own.

It is funny how the discovery of a dream, passion or purpose emerges. It can be a beautiful and messy experience. Sometimes it is discovered by accident. Or through a process of life elimination (different jobs, to find it's not something you want to do). For some people, it comes through divine revelation (part of the case in my experience). Or simply reconnecting with a long-lost love of something you used to do. However it reveals itself is always a wonderful thing. It is just embracing and making it a reality that can be the tricky part.

So, how do you start to follow your dreams? There is no one-size-fits-all answer that applies to everyone. Why? Because we all have different circumstances and situations unique to us, that lead us to a purposeful path. Yet, there are three things that anyone can do to build a framework to lay hold of it in due course:

Capture your dream

Write down the thing you want to do. Or you can create a vision board and visually capture it. I have done both. I have found that writing down my dreams, helps me to be sure of what I want to do. It is like I am setting it in stone.

Plan

Once you have captured it, brainstorm about it. What steps would it take to achieve it? Also, it is good to add a layer of accountability, by giving yourself a timescale of when to do things. It will remind you and keep you on track for what you want to achieve.

Have courage

This is where the action comes in. It is one thing to have a dream and a plan, but you *must* have courage. Make that phone call. Apply for that course or job. Visit the places you want to be in and imagine living your dream. You must follow through with action. Otherwise, your dream will remain a dream.

There will never be a perfect time to start anything. So, it is better to start today. Your dream may seem impossible now; but if you start by taking small steps, you will be closer than it was yesterday.

Delight yourself in the Lord, and he will give you the desires of your heart. **Psalm 37:4**

Personal Development

What does personal improvement mean to you? Let me frame it another way: what does personal development look like in your life? Take a moment to consider the question. Because many people do not think about personal development. A lot of people assume personal development naturally comes with age. This is not true. Just because you get older, or taller with each birthday, does not mean you naturally progress emotionally, mentally, and intellectually. Personal development is an intentional pursuit. What tends to happen as some people get older, is personal development is not pursued. As a matter of fact, for many people, personal development was never a priority in the first place. But it should be a priority. Why? Because it's about you. Personal development is about raising the bar for yourself. Optimising everything about you, your health, and your personal knowledge.

According to market data, the self-improvement industry is worth 11.3 billion dollars in 2021. That means that for the many people not pursuing personal development activities, there are many others who are undertaking the journey. My personal development journey started after working through past issues. Initially at 22yrs old, working through childhood issues, but at 35yrs old, I started to take it seriously. You see, the journey of personal development/self-improvement is a gradual one, of small steps. I started with small things: losing weight, deciding what goals I wanted to achieve, and most important of all, discovering and following my God-given purpose in my life.

Maybe you have never thought about personal development or self-development before. Or maybe you›ve been trying to develop yourself, but keep giving up because you're not seeing the results you had hoped for. Maybe you say to yourself 'if it isn't broken why fix it?' Meaning, you are comfortable and don›t want to be stretched, to do something new to better yourself. The question you need to ask yourself is: are you sure you don›t want to explore your potential? Are you sure you are going to be happy in five, ten, or fifteen-years' time, with the result of not growing or evolving as a person? I don›t really believe anyone wants that. Obviously, there are people out there with a fixed mindset mentality, but I believe if you desire to do the things you dream of, or want to be a better version of yourself, you want to develop.

Personal development involves inner and outer work, on the mind and body using resources, services, and other things to help you achieve the desired goal. So many things can mask the need for personal development. From my personal experience, supporting women in my non-profit organisation *Daughter Arise* for the last decade and through my empowerment coaching conversations and observation with clients, sometimes people cannot see room for development because 'stuff' is in the way. That 'stuff' could be unresolved issues, trauma, habits, or comfort. Other times, people do not know personal development is what they need, because they are not aware of what it entails or its benefits. Sometimes people don't know what you need, because other things need to happen first. It was only when my stuff was stripped away that I could clearly see the areas of me that need working on.

So, if you are someone who wants to be exceptional and not expected, to live an empowered life; understand that personal development is a huge part of it. Top areas of personal development: Mental, social, spiritual, emotional, physical, and education. I want to share with you some questions to ask yourself and some tips on areas where you can get some quick wins, meaning areas that are not too difficult to get started.

Questions to ask yourself:

What are your life goals?

What things do you want to improve about yourself as a person?

What areas about you and your life have you neglected?

What do you want to achieve?

These questions act as guides to help you identify areas of personal development and help decide the steps needed to be the best to get there and achieve it.

Personal development quick wins:

Reflection

Build Knowledge

Try new things

Deal with trauma

Learn from mistakes

Resources to help you on your journey:

Books

Podcasts

Workshops

Coaching

Online courses

Mentoring

Also, Google is your best friend; search for what you need, or if you have friends or family who are doing personal development stuff, ask them questions about how it's going, and where to find support. You can also visit my company website, YEME Empowerment, for personal development resources. If there are parts of your life that you feel you cannot change, know that with God, you can. Give your life to Christ and he will help you transform your life. With him, you can live your best life.

For with God nothing will be impossible. **Luke 1:37**

Purpose in the Pain

Painful experiences can be life-changing – they can make or break you. For a long time, I was mentally, emotionally, and spiritually broken by childhood sexual abuse. And, for a long time, I thought I would never recover, let alone find purpose in the pain.

For years I felt voiceless and powerless to change my life. Rejection, humiliation, betrayal, and depression left me broken. I had two mental breakdowns in my twenties and both times I thought there was no hope. That was until I found my voice.

I wrote my autobiography *Daughter Arise* as a way of voicing all the things I could not say; the things that no one wanted to hear. It was my statement and testimony to the world, detailing what I experienced and how through Jesus Christ, I overcame the aftermath of abuse. This step of courage started a chain of events that I did not expect. Strangers felt comfortable enough to share their own pain and secrets with me, after hearing my story. It was surreal to realise that I empowered and helped people by finding my voice – it birthed my purpose. The book led me to become the founder of a non-profit organisation that offers peer empowerment to other survivors, subsequently leading to other opportunities: speaking events, other events, and workshops. My pain seemed to be the gift that keeps on giving! Moreover, I discovered I had the gift of empowering others to make positive life changes through my skills, talents, and life experiences. I could help people become unstuck because *I* was once stuck in so many areas of my life, and it was evidenced in how I overcame adversity.

A leader or a person of influence, is best equipped to help others when they have actually experienced what others have gone through. To help people overcome their issues, I had to overcome mine. There was a process I had to go through, and it involved different things: forgiveness, therapy, and self-acceptance. I want to share with you some lessons I learnt on the journey from pain to purpose.

It was painful and unpleasant but totally necessary

Just as the female body goes through a process to prepare to give birth to a baby, I had to go through a process to prepare myself to use the pain of my experiences for a greater purpose. I had to face my trauma, the humiliation, and the betrayal of all that I endured, and deal with and heal in every aspect of it. Had I not gone through the process, I certainly would not have been able to help other people on a similar journey, or recognise my God-given purpose. Giving birth to my purpose was a long and painful process. I remember the pain I experienced in giving birth to my two daughters. It was unpleasant but necessary to birth my beautiful girls. My body had to go through all the stages to develop my babies in the womb. Likewise, I could never have given birth to my purpose, if I didn't go through the stages to experience all the amazing things I am doing today.

What I experienced was not about me

I know it may seem a weird thing to say, but I feel that the things I experienced were for a cause greater than me. I am not saying my abuse should have happened to me, but God turned the evil meant against me for good (Genesis 50:20). The reality of life, is that we have the freedom to make good and bad choices; that is the beauty and reality of free will. My dad made a decision that affected my life for twenty-five years. I dealt with the consequences and suffered for it. The fact that I overcame so much adversity, means I can help people suffering abuse or challenging life issues, to find a way out and provide knowledge and resources to help. If I hadn't been through those experiences, I would not have been able to support people with those same difficulties. For twelve years, I have been empowering and encouraging people via various endeavours, such as *Daughter Arise* and my company YEME Empowerment, a facility that empowers people through resources and services.

Finding purpose in the pain allowed me to connect authentically with myself

I know my limits; I know my boundaries. I know my weaknesses and my strengths. I know where I've come from, and I know where I am going. I know why God has put me on earth, and I know the groups of people I am here to empower and inspire. My mission is to bring the vision and call God has on my life to reality, and walk in its fullness. Pain allowed me to know myself mentally, emotionally, and spiritually. Dr Rob Yeung author of the book, *Confidence* says: *'Some of life's most valuable lessons and opportunities really are disguised as setbacks at the time.* I have discovered this to be true. What was meant to destroy me, propelled me to my purpose. At the time, I did not recognise it, but as I overcame each pain point, I realised that something could be utilised from it.

I want you to know that your troubling, painful or challenging life experiences are not in vain; they could well be to prepare you for something else. If you have been through difficult experiences, I want to encourage you to think about what you can glean from them. It could be something you have learned about yourself or from the situation. It could be that it has changed your perspective on life. Is there one thing you can take away that can empower you? Do not let pain be the purpose. Instead, find purpose in the pain.

The spirit of the Sovereign Lord is upon me, he has anointed me to proclaim good news to the poor. To bestow on them a crown of beauty instead of ashes. (Isaiah 61: 1-3)

Push Through Hard Challenges

I have experienced many complex challenges throughout my lifetime. Some of them I was sure I would not overcome. Moreover, each challenge had unique circumstances that I had to navigate whilst feeling overwhelmed, stressed, and uncertain of what to do to get through it. One thing I have come to discover: life is full of challenges – it is inevitable.

Recently I completed another challenge; my first essay for my Innovation Management and Entrepreneurship master's degree. Over eighty hours of study and research were undertaken, something I have never done before. It was stressful and hard. I can admit I cried a couple of times. I nearly quit. However, I found a way to do it. I watched videos, bought, and read books, and accessed coaching help from the university. I pushed through one step and one day at a time. I am happy that I figured out a strategy. A quote by anonymous says; 'strength grows in the moments when you think you can't go on, but you keep going anyway.'
And it is true. In those moments I discovered:

Fear will always be present when you are doing new things

It has a purpose: to deter you from pushing through hard challenges. To stop you from exploring new pursuits. Fear is the ultimate deceiver. It is a false flag, because fear says this is a sign; stop whatever it is you are attempting to do. Fear is a normal response to facing new things. I thought I would fail my essay because I had never done one before. Yet I pushed through the lies of fear, and on the other side, I received a pass with merit (one tier down from a distinction grade) for my essay. Never listen to lies of fear. The, 'too old', 'not good enough', 'not smart enough' lies. Go forward and pursue what you want to do anyway – do not worry about the outcome.

If you want it bad enough, you will find a way to do it

I did an all-nighter (staying up all through the night) to get my assignment done. Something I have not done since the raving days of my early twenties! However, I was determined to do it and my determination provided the strength I needed to get the work done. Additionally, learning from others resulted in me adopting their methods and approach to make writing the essay easier. Sometimes you must find a way to get through it, over it or under it. I kept in mind why I was doing it, and what I wanted to achieve. Everything in between was the steps to get there.

Challenges are character-building exercises

I learned this from other life challenges. However, it was good to be reminded again. In the moments when I felt unsure that I could complete the essay, that I could not find the strength to push through, something was happening in the background; my character was being built. ***Tests and trials will either make us or break us.*** It is up to us what we choose. My challenges have made me the woman I am today. I am fortunate that they have helped me become resilient. On the plus side, challenges can help us do things we have not done before. I now know how to write academically, research and put together a piece of work to a high standard. If you are currently trying to push through hard challenges, remember you first win the battle before you win the war. Start by:

Taking a step back to assess the situation

It will help you to decide the best strategy to take and help you to break down the challenge into manageable steps.

Find resources to help you

Knowledge is power, and it comes in various forms. Find what works for you and apply it to the situation.

Take it one step at-a-time, one day at-a-time

Try not to face your challenges in one go, especially without tools or support to help you; you will become overwhelmed, and it can lead to discouragement. No matter what happens push through your hard challenges. Don't give up or give in. You will overcome.

No temptation has overtaken you that is not common to man. God is faithful, and he will not let you be tempted beyond your ability, but with temptation, he will also provide a way of escape, so that you may be able to endure it. **1 Corinthians 10:13**

Small Step Success

Small steps, even though they seem insignificant are actually the most important part of achieving your goals. There is a quote that says, 'it's the journey, not the destination.' And it is true. People are so focused on the end goal – the pinnacle of whatever success is for them – that nothing else matters. They are keen to get to their destination; and you know that is all well and good BUT it is not the most important part of the process– the steps to get there are.

What›s really sad is that I have seen people remain stuck for years, *decades* even, because they don't like small steps and they refuse to take them, because they believe they should be able to complete their goal with one try. All this mindset does, is keep them from taking action. Disregarding the significance of small steps is damaging to a person who wants to achieve things in their life.

For example, a lady that I know struggled to do things in her home. She was overwhelmed by the task for years. Eventually, she did it and was proud of her achievement. However, she could not appreciate the result of her efforts or bask in the glory of her moment, because she was focused on what she had *not* done. She beat herself up because of the time it took her to start, and what she could have done better. No matter what I said to congratulate her, she couldn't see the enormity of her small step of progress. Sometimes, because of our own standards and expectations, small progress is often overlooked.

I can understand it though. I used to be someone who only acknowledged big strides of progress, rather than the small steps. Yet when I was struggling with depression, low self-esteem and low confidence, I appreciated any step; small steps of change, progress and achievement – it meant so much to me. I didn›t take it for granted. However, as I started to achieve more, the small steps were not enough and I began to look to the big steps for validation of my work and evidence of success. I ended up feeling discouraged; not content with where I was in my life and feeling that what I was doing was not enough.

On reflection, I think I stopped appreciating how amazing it was to come from where I came from and the steps it took to get there. I started to feel pressurised, because my disadvantages, setbacks from dealing with trauma and other issues, caused a twenty-five-year delay in my life. I felt I needed to make big strides to catch up with others who were doing things at the same stage of life; but I wasn›t being fair to myself. I wasn›t considering what I had battled through or that those other people I used as a benchmark for where *I* should be in life, might not have had the same challenges as me. I thought I could run the race the same as the next person, who had not been through the journey I had. I now understand that small steps of progress are okay and that I need to be kind to myself. I understand and appreciate small steps of progress, and their significance in my overall journey. I understand I can do only what I can do and to stop putting pressure on myself.

It is easy to dismiss your small steps of progress because it›s not the full achievement or completion of your goals. But there is a process to progress – and that comes in the form of steps; taking one day at a time. So, you can start to appreciate small steps of progress by:

Congratulation on your achievements

Do not reject anything you have managed to do, because in doing so you are rejecting yourself.

Remember where you were so you can appreciate where you are now

Understand that your small steps are part of the bigger picture. Enjoy it as part of your journey.

Do not despise small beginnings for the Lord rejoices to see the work begin. **Zechariah 4:10**

Your Unique
Power Is Your
VOICE Never Let
Anyone Silence It

Stay on Code

An essential part of being exceptional and not expected, is to live a life true to God and yourself. Many people find it hard to do and they are easily swayed and influenced by others, because they have no foundation or grounding, and this usually arises from low self-esteem and confidence which results in people-pleasing, conforming to social pressure and the need to be liked.

One of the things that I did not know was a strength of mine – I am strongminded. It is a trait that helped me not to recant on telling someone about my sexual abuse as a child, when my family ostracised me. A family member told me to apologise, but I stood by the truth and stayed true to myself. Many times, when various social, work and family situations have called for me to compromise myself, beliefs, or morals I stood my ground.

People who are not on code with themselves (true to their beliefs, morals, life purpose, and individuality) are easily swayed and moved out of position, because the foundation of who they are is not established. I believe the foundation, guidance, and strength to stay on code and be true to myself comes from the Living God through Jesus, who is the way, the truth, and the life (John 14:6). Through his Holy Spirit, God reveals all truth. To live on code, requires recognising your wrongs (sin) and that you need the forgiveness of God. Also, to recognise the need for the grace of God and accept the gift of salvation as a gift from Jesus Christ. To stay on code, I believe, is to have the right foundation in Him. It is essential to navigating the influences and ways of the world. We as humans are fallible, that›s why we need Jesus. Yet, even in our shortcomings we can stand tall and live true to the life God purposed for each of us. He is all that I have needed to live on code; He helps me not to bend to the persuasion and influence of others.

How to stay on code with yourself:

Ask Jesus into your heart and life.

Live an intentional life (this comes through knowing the purpose of your life, and once you know, it then becomes a process of eliminating everything that does not fall in line with it.

Have standards about yourself and only do things that reinforce and stay true to your code.

Do not people please, or look to others for validation (that includes social media).

Therefore, whoever hears these sayings of Mine, and does them, I will liken him to a wise man who built his house on the rock: 2 and the rain descended, the floods came, and the winds blew and beat on that house; and it did not fall, for it was founded on the rock. **Matthew 7:24**

Take a Risk

I had the pleasure of interviewing Natasha Rego on the *Living the Empowered Life* podcast. Tasha has been influential in my journey of courage. She was the only person I knew back in 2013 that had left a traditional, secure paid job, to start her own business based on an idea she had. So, when I was about to embark on a similar journey in 2016, it was natural for me to ask her for advice. Inspired by her courage, I left my secure job eighteen months later, to set up my own company YEME Empowerment. There are some things I was reminded of during our conversation, about taking a risk to try and do something new or different:

Firstly, there is never a right time.

Secondly, you must sacrifice something.

Lastly, even with the challenges, there is freedom.

There were many valuable takeaways from what Tasha shared. But the message was clear; take a risk and give whatever you want to do a try. The thing about risk is that you cannot sit on the fence of indecision. Because that is where procrastination, doubt, delay, unhappiness, and fear will meet you. You must decide 'yes' or 'no'. There are different ways you can take a risk. Some options can be done alongside other things. But it all starts with what you decide.

So, as you continue to journey through life, I want to encourage you to take a risk. Give that class a try. Do that new hobby. Work on your side hustle. Apply for a job that is very different from what you do. What is the worst that can happen? You will never know until you give it a try.

Dream big and fly high. Life is for living.

Enlarge the place of your tent, stretch your tent curtains wide, do not hold back; lengthen your cords, and strengthen your stakes. **Isaiah 54:2**

The Benefit of Life Experience

Some life experiences are understood with time. Others are not; we may never get answers in this lifetime. We may not have got what resolution, or result we hoped for out of the situation, or circumstance, but that does not mean, that the encountered experience was of no value at all. You see, that is another key part of being exceptional and expected and living an empowered life: using life experiences to empower ourselves and others, especially if the experience was disempowering and we found a way to overcome it.

Since 2010 I have shared my life experiences openly and honestly through different resources; books, social media, and YouTube; the good, the bad and the ugly. I have also shared – through evidence of my life in action – how I have used my life experiences to empower, educate, inspire, and motivate others. The benefits of doing so far outweigh the momentary pain, disappointment, and heartache that I felt about life at the time. I am reminded of the donkey in the well story. Basically, the donkey owner put the donkey in the well and shovelled dirt into it to bury the donkey. However, the Donkey used the dirt to climb out of the well. In essence, that is what I have done with certain situations in life that have tried to bury me – I used them to my advantage.

If you are struggling with the experiences you have had in life, I want to tell you that there are benefits you can glean from them. Some of the positives are:

They can grow, strengthen, and develop you. The trials of life can build your character and strength. Adversity prepares you for situations that are yet to come.

They can teach you important lessons (whether good or bad). Life is a teacher. Knowledge is taught in places other than school. Life experience is diverse and can speak to people regardless of race, sex, or religion.

The things you've learned through life lessons, you can impart that knowledge to others. Your lived experience is invaluable. People are more likely to listen to someone who's been there and done that. You can be an influence for good. I have found this to be true. People are more likely to appreciate and believe someone who has first-hand experience with the subject they are speaking about. You automatically have authority because you've been through it and lived it.

Never let anyone make you feel 'less than', for the experiences that you have had or how you have dealt with the outcomes. Even if you were the catalyst in those experiences, or just dealing with the hand life dealt you. Good can come from perceived bad. The key is to own those experiences because in doing so, you gain empowerment.

Wisdom is with aged men, and with length of days, understanding. **Job 12:12**

The Benefit of Mastering Self

There are many benefits to mastering self. However, it is not a subject that most people think about, especially in these terms. Admittedly, I never gave it much thought until I was well into my personal development journey in my mid-thirties. But as I got to learn what it entails, I have embraced it as a valuable addition to enhance my life.

For many years, because of childhood sexual abuse, I was an emotionally led, and at times impulsive person. Childhood trauma led me to believe I had no control or rights over myself and this transcended into other areas of my life. However, once I realised that I had control over my thoughts, feelings, choices, and decisions, it was a life changer for me. My new dimension of self-discovery encouraged me to know myself better. One of the main benefits that self-mastery has brought into my life, is helping me to set standards and boundaries in what I will and will not allow.

Self-mastery means being in control of you; your choices, decisions, and feelings. It is about not allowing outside influences to dictate who you are or what you do. At the core of self-mastery is self-awareness.

Benefits of mastering self:

Empowers you

Self-mastery can help you to take ownership of yourself. Rather than let life live you, you will live your life.

Help you to live a fulfilled life

Nothing is better than knowing and understanding your weaknesses, strengths, and capabilities. Imagine yourself as a car filled with the best petrol to optimise performance. This is what self-mastery brings to your life. It is the inner knowledge that will help you live the best life you can.

It provides a framework to define the type of life you want

It is your inner compass. Your boundaries. Feelings, choices, and decisions will be influenced and guided by it.

I am still learning about self-mastery. It is something that takes time to develop and is cultivated over a lifetime. One thing I have found to be true, is that we can only master ourselves and not others. However, self-mastery does allow a boundary of respect to be built with yourself and others. Let it be a pillar of personal strength in your life.

But the fruit of the spirit is love, joy, peace, forbearance, kindness, goodness, faithfulness, gentleness, and self-control. Against such a thing there is not law. **Galatians 5:22-23 (NIV)**

The Biggest Critic

Criticism, unfortunately, is something at one point or another in our lives that we all experience. Usually, it comes from those around us: friends, family, colleagues, and acquaintances, and is connected to something we have done, or a decision or choice that we made. However, what if I told you that the biggest critic is most often ourselves. Why? Because we know our insecurities, shortcomings, and weaknesses. The inner critic also rears its ugly head through fear, doubt, low self-esteem, and lack of confidence. It is self-criticism, negative self-talk, and harsh thoughts towards self.

The inner critic is naturally within all of us to a degree. However, its voice is magnified and becomes loud in everything that we do, unless it is transformed into something we can use as power. The inner critic can become self-condemnation. Its trait can be recognised when it highlights *problems* not *solutions* to a challenge. It derails you from doing stuff, or when you try, it diminishes your efforts, saying that you should have done better, and why didn't you do X Y Z. It never celebrates – but rather debilitates. Inner criticism is a negative force unless reined in through empowerment.

To handle the inner critic:

Compliment yourself on the things that you have done well. When it comes in for the attack, don't feed it with more self-criticism; drown it in self-kindness.

Treat the inner critic as you would when someone else gives you negative feedback. Take what you can use and discard the rest. Use it as inner guidance.

Don't let the inner critic defeat you. Use it to your advantage to help you do things better, or to give you a different perspective.

Remember, the inner critic comes from you, not outside sources. You have the power to change what it says. You have the power to quieten its voice by showing yourself grace and being compassionate towards yourself.

For God did not send His Son into the world to condemn the world, but that the world through Him might be saved. **John 3:17**

The Characteristics of a plan A Person

A plan A person never has a plan B. They may be tempted to consider other options when situations are shaky or challenging, or when feeling doubtful or fearful, but they will hold on to the vision of what they are hoping for, because it is better than what they experienced before. I used to be a plan B, C and D person until I discovered God's purpose for my life.

I learned to be a plan A person through a relationship with Jesus Christ. It did not happen overnight; I had to learn to trust God and put my confidence in him with everything. A plan A person does not live on the opinions of others; they are individuals who are comfortable in their own skin. They dance to the beat of their own drum and are comfortable with their decisions – even if they make mistakes. I want to share with you from my experience what I believe are some of the characteristics, hallmarks, and attributes of a plan A person:
Live by faith.

Trusts in God.

Does not get distracted by people's opinions and feelings.

Purpose-driven.

Are all or nothing.

Risk takers.

Single-minded.

Focused on their goal.

Know their own mind and are not easily led.

Not double-minded.

Faith in God is the foundation on which the plan A person builds everything else. It does require courage to hold your resolve and stick with what you believe when everything is screaming that you are going in the wrong direction, or that you have made the wrong choice, but great freedom comes as the reward.

Now faith is the substance of things hoped for, the evidence of things not seen. **Hebrews 11:1**

The First Step is Always the Hardest

I have done a lot of things for the first time. As mentioned, I released my third book; the first in a different genre. I created my first online course and started a podcast. Also, I did my first in-conversation interview on my YouTube channel – Living the Empowered Life. I have found this to be true in all new experiences – the first step is always the hardest.

For example, interviewing guests on my YouTube channel. I had been meaning to do this for some time, but I kept putting it off. I procrastinated about it – I don›t know why. Conducting interviews is not a new experience for me. Back in 2007, I worked as an Interview Officer for the U.K. passport service for five years. It was quite a repetitive, but important job. I interviewed people from all walks of life, who were applying for their first British passports. I never imagined that the skills I acquired from that job, would be used outside of this specialist role. Yet here I am years later, using it creatively to interview guests on my channel.

So, what helped me to take the first step? I just decided to push through my fear and go for it; with the help of prayer, creativity, my previous interview skills, and belief in myself. I am so glad I did it. It was not as bad as I thought it would be. And over time, I developed my communication techniques to become better at it.

Are you considering trying something for the first time? Here are three things you need to know about taking the first step:

Feel the fear and do it anyway

Joyce Meyer, a famous author uses this quote often. Fear and discomfort will always be present when attempting something new. It is part and parcel of taking the first step into the unknown. It's easy to let fear get in the way of what you want to do. But you must go for it anyway. Anything worth having in life will involve some type of personal cost.

The first step requires courage

Courage builds confidence. Confidence is built after taking the first step. Once you have done it, you will find the other steps are not as scary. Of course, there will be challenges to overcome, but you will figure it out. Be courageous and see what happens.

The first step provides an opportunity to learn

After you take the first step, you can make changes, learn from mistakes, and redefine your goal if you need to. Seize the opportunity that the first step will teach you today.

Without the first step, procrastination and fear will keep you bound. There is never a perfect time to do it. Put your best foot forward! Something new awaits you.

If you wait for perfect conditions, you will never get anything done. **Ecclesiastes 11:4**

The Self-Sabotage Struggle

Have you ever struggled with self-sabotage? You know when things are going well for you in a particular area, and you railroad yourself? You start well, have a bad day, thoughts trigger, and then self-sabotage shows up and shows out... And ruins your efforts! Self-sabotage has been a major struggle in my life and is counterproductive to living an empowered life. I have self-sabotaged – diets on my weight management journey, accepting love in a relationship, in areas I know I deserve better. Not feeling worthy of love was a trigger for self-sabotage early on in my marriage. I used to sabotage things with my husband (arguments, etc) and push him away. I didn't feel I was worthy to receive love because... well... I didn't feel that I was loveable and didn't believe I deserved love. And because of my background, (childhood trauma, living in a family where love was not openly demonstrated positively) I did not recognise that love was openly shared and that it was not meant to be painful. There are many reasons people self-sabotage. From my experience and in my many conversations with people who have experienced the same thing, three common reasons were mentioned: Lack of self-discipline and focus, self-worth issues, and believing they are worthy of the things they desire.

I also believe self-sabotage comes into play when you fear the thing you want to change or do. You›ve been used to something for so long, used to its comfort, that the fear of a new routine or way of doing things makes you feel fear, and as you take a step deeper into the unknown you think ‹ooh this is scary›, the desire for familiarity shows up and then the cycle of self-sabotage begins. To ease the struggle of self-sabotage, I believe this is where self-worth comes in. Believing you are enough regardless of the outcomes you want, goes a long way. Knowing that you show up and try is enough and that everything else is a bonus, alleviates self-sabotage. John Niland in his book *The Self-Worth Safari* talks about self-esteem and how creating conditions on self is the nemesis to the journey of self-acceptance and worth. To be loved by someone who won't hurt you can feel intimidating and make you feel vulnerable. Believing you deserve to give yourself a chance to have opportunities, experiences, or things you've never dreamed of before can make you think 'who am I to think I can have this?' Maybe it is because you've never aimed higher, hence you feel undeserving. I just want to tell you that these feelings are normal. Railroading the good things destined only harms you. Self-sabotage is not the answer.

To avoid the self-sabotage struggle:

Take each day as it comes; take one step at a time. Set realistic goals. Unrealistic goals will make you feel overwhelmed and cause you to have a setback which can sabotage what you are trying to do, so start small.

Try and tune in to your sabotage triggers. What is it that happens just BEFORE you sabotage? Is it tiredness, or negative thoughts? In recognising the pitfalls beforehand, you can try and put things in place to help you before a situation arises.

Get support from someone you trust. Let them be your accountability partner. It could also mean going to a therapist to get help to understand what makes you self-sabotage. Therapy really helped me to understand the roots of the things that were hindering me.

A transformation of mindset through acquiring knowledge, understanding your worth, identifying and finding solutions to your triggers and empowerment and help from the Living God can help you with the challenges of self-sabotage. You don't have to stay stuck in the cycle. I know the frustration, shame, and disappointment it can bring, but it is not permanent. It may feel like it will always keep you bound but you can break it.

God is our refuge and strength. A very present help in times of trouble. **Psalm 46:1**

The Thing About Mountains

In general, when people think about mountains, usually the vision is synonymous with big, overwhelming, and impossible. However, at some point or time in life, we have all faced a personal mountain. These mountains can be personal problems, challenges, tests, or trials. During my life, I have experienced many personal mountains; financial, family, and mental health mountains. One of the things I realised when reflecting on these mountains, is that what seems insurmountable, can be overcome. Even transitioning from career to calling felt like a mountain that would defeat me. As I shared this with my friend Andrena, who I interviewed on my YouTube channel *Living the Empowered Life*, we both found it to be a normal part of undertaking this mountain challenge.

What I realised about mountains, is that if you spend too much time focusing on them, they will leave you feeling helpless and discouraged. Instead of thinking about solutions to tackle the problem, I focused on the problem. This resulted in me having a lot of negative thoughts. I had to go back to basics by focusing on God. I prayed and asked him for help to keep my eyes on him, not my problems. After all, he is a way-maker (Isaiah 43:16). Also, I noticed two specific things about mountains. First, you cannot move a mountain by focusing on it. Second, mountains are the training ground to build resilience. Admittedly, it is hard not to allow challenges or problems to consume you, but you must take it one day at a time. Not too long ago, I came through the rough terrain of the pandemic mountain and the summit (the top, the end) was in sight. Now I am starting to reflect on what I have learned, so that I can glean from this experience, knowledge, insights, or tips to help me face the next mountain. Because as we go through this journey called life, we will always experience them. If you look at mountaineers, they prepare to mountain climb. They research the terrain and select the equipment they need – and most importantly, they devise a plan. As the saying goes: *preparation is the key to success.*

To conquer your mountain, you need a plan. A strategy to win one step at a time. You will need tools and resources to empower yourself and positive reminders of the mountains you have overcome. At the back of this book, you will see different resources I have included to encourage and support you. So, I encourage you to:

Focus on God

Tell him about your cares and worries. All the things you are finding challenging. Ask him to reveal himself to you, and he will. Also, ask him for solutions to your problems. He is an ever-present help in times of trouble.

Focus on the things you can change

Rather than focus on what is keeping you stuck, how about looking at the things you can have a hand in changing?

Reflect on the times you overcame other mountains

Do you remember the times when you thought you would never get through a previous trial, challenge, or problem but you did? Use these times to encourage you.

Remember, you can overcome your mountains. You can and will conquer them. It is only a matter of time. And that by the grace of God is something you have on your side.

What is impossible with man is possible with God: **(Luke 18:27)**

The Trade-Off

Living the Empowered Life is about you living your life to its fullest potential and purpose. It entails being God-empowered and spirit-led. It is about living a life of value. Creating good memories and having new experiences. It means living a life of gratitude and a life of peace. It is about living life tailored to you, not tailored to the demands of others and the world around you. It is totally your right to have, but many people find they must fight for the right to have it.

And yes, you must fight for it. However, I didn't realise when I stepped out four years ago that the battle would be so hard. At times it felt like an impossible thing to do. It certainly involved a lot of learning, reflection, re-direction, prayer, and resolve. Without God, I don't think I would have endured the hard times I have experienced. I gave up the comfort of known circumstances, for the unknown of the different experiences of life. I gave up a traditional career path, to be a creative entrepreneur. I gave up corporate stress for inner peace; the trade-off has been worth it.

The trade-off means different things to different people. I sat down for a chat with a lady named Hasu, for an episode of *Living the Empowered Life* podcast. She decided to leave a job that she loved during the pandemic. Not to pursue a more prestigious career or extra money, it was to have new life experiences and to do things she is passionate about. Hasu's trade-off? She exchanged the feeling of restrictiveness for happiness. Less money to explore life. Virtual isolation (during the pandemic, her role involved a lot of Ms Teams) for connection with people and nature.

Anyone seeking to live an empowered life, will need to know sacrifices will have to be made. The trade-off is never easy, and the question you need to ask yourself is: is it worth it? If you are thinking of making some trade-offs in your life, here are some things to consider:

Write down the pros and cons

Your list could be the positives and negatives. The benefits, or the disadvantages. Think about what is important and meaningful to you.

Evaluate your life

Taking stock of your life will help you to decipher whether your current choices and decisions up until this point have been worth it. Also, it will help you recognise what you need to spend more time on (or less) and whether change is long overdue.

Listen to your heart

It is always worth listening to. A lot of the time, we make decisions with our heads because we want to be sensible and responsible. However, I have found in my experience some of the best decisions I made have involved my heart. This usually means it doesn't make sense to others, but it makes total sense to you. Taking a risk never usually leads from the head, but from the heart.

Whatever you trade-off, make sure it is worth the sacrifice because it may cost you in another area. However, it is a small price to pay for the value you will gain from your decision.

Now the Lord is a spirit, and where the spirit of the Lord is there is freedom. **2 Corinthians 3:17**

Past Success Is Future Motivation

The Trolley Experience

An ex-colleague and friend inspired me many years ago, with her story about a trolley! Melanie recalled a time as a young lady in her early twenties, after a lively night out, when she climbed into a supermarket trolley. It was a spur-of-the-moment decision; one that led to her being pushed home in the trolley by her friends. Her face lit up as she reminisced with fondness and told me the story. I found it extremely funny, because many people would probably not believe from Melanie's outer appearance and demeanour that she would do something like that. But I was not surprised as she is a fun-loving person. What made this story funnier, was at the time, we were both working in a job that was anything but a trolley experience; it was boring, mundane, and comfortable. Fortunately, I left that job at forty-one years old to step into the unknown to start my own business. And Melanie, at the time in her late fifties, left her job a few months after me to pursue a job better suited to the way she wanted to live her life. Both of us wanted to do something new – both of us seeking a trolley experience.

So, what is a trolley experience? *It simply means to do something new, different, or exciting; a chance to do something unexpected and courageous.* **To do something that interrupts the rhythm of life.**

Because let's face it, life will become repetitive if you allow it to. As we grow through the cycle of life, 'adulting' does not openly present many opportunities for a trolley experience. Those moments of taking risks and letting go of thinking through every step of our decisions, are usually done with hesitancy and careful planning. To be careful, not carefree, is what the traditional way of life shapes us to become. Of course, everything is in good measure. But the danger is, we become laden with the cares of life rather than seizing the opportunity to live in the moment. When was the last time you did something exciting, out of the ordinary or new? If you cannot remember, here are three tips to help you get in your trolley:

Keep your mind open to the possibility of new experiences

Do not close yourself down to trying new things because of your age or circumstances. Try and see if you can do something new or different every day. Just taking a different route to work is something different!

Look for opportunities to do things you have never done before

Try that Zumba class you have always wanted to do. If you have a talent, showcase it to others. Whatever you have wanted to do, give it a go.

Say 'no' to fear and 'yes' to courage

Fear will keep you from your trolley experience. As a matter of fact, fear will convince you to stick with what you know. Do not let fear, doubt, or anything else get in your way.

To do things that are not planned is totally okay. Take the opportunity to have a trolley experience and do something that is not the status quo. Never let circumstances or your age be reasons to stop you. May the memories of your trolley experience fuel more adventures!

You will show me the path of life; In Your presence is fullness of joy; At Your right hand are pleasures forevermore. **Psalm 16:11**

Three Life Lessons Marriage Taught Me

I celebrated my seventeenth wedding anniversary in 2022. It is by no means a small feat, and as a matter of fact, we both laughed that we have made it this far. I am proud of this achievement, considering the background I came from. I have learned a lot about myself; love, and communication, plus many other things. I want to share with you three life lessons marriage has taught me, that I hope will encourage you:

Perseverance pays off

I can remember between years eight and thirteen in marriage being the hardest. At times I felt sure we would not make it through all the challenges we were experiencing. However, we talked, argued, pushed our way through the difficult times and persevered. If you are facing situations that feel hopeless, that are extremely hard – do not quit. If you can push through and hold on, you will find that something greater is on the other side of the storm.

Change starts with self

In the earlier years of my relationship, I nagged my husband about things I didn't like. My efforts were counterproductive and did not lead to the changes I had hoped for. With the wisdom and knowledge, I gained over the years, I learned that it is more effective, impactful, and influential for my husband to witness me work on myself. It encouraged my husband to change. The saying 'you catch more bees with honey than with vinegar' is true. I cannot change my husband; I can only change myself. I discovered the power of leading by example. People are more likely to be inspired and motivated by witnessing *your* change in action, rather than telling *them* what to do. If you want people around you to change, be the change you would like to see. For instance, if they communicate with you in a way you find difficult, communicate with them in the way you would like. Hopefully, it will influence them to communicate better with you. Remember, change starts with self. It is holding yourself accountable. When others see it, it gives them little room for excuse.

Teamwork is key

Marriage never works well with selfish intentions. This is a lesson both of us learnt (years later!). The best image I can give you to envision, is two boats trying to dock alongside each other. The boats must follow the same instructions to get the desired result. It won't work if both boats want to steer their own way. This is what marriage is like. We need to work together with communication and cooperation to get the best outcome, to achieve a better relationship and our family goals. It will not work if we are doing our own thing. This aspect in particular, has been a painful lesson to learn. It took years to finally understand that we achieve more together than working apart. Whether in marriage, work, or relationships in general, teamwork really makes the dream work! Learning to be a team player will benefit you and others. Keep in mind the end goal – it will help to make it easier.

Living an empowered life and being exceptional and not expected, means that when life brings us lessons, we learn and apply them. After all, life is enriched by all our experiences – good or bad.

Not only so, but we also glory in our sufferings, because we know that suffering produces perseverance; perseverance, character; and character, hope. And hope does not put us to shame, because God's love has been poured out into our hearts through the Holy Spirit, who has been given to us. **Romans 5:3-5**

Time to Say Goodbye

The truth is, you cannot say hello and embrace the new, whilst holding on to and not saying goodbye to things that are holding you back from being exceptional and not expected. A common reason a lot of people do not recognise when it's time to say goodbye to someone or something, is because of the comfort that thing brings. Other people do recognise it's time to say goodbye, but find it hard to let go. Goodbyes come in different ways. It could be saying goodbye to a relationship, friendship, job, habit, or way of life. Sometimes, goodbye doesn't happen by choice. Sometimes circumstances initiate it – for instance when someone dies.

I remember one of the hardest goodbyes I have ever had to face in my life; when I was taken into care by social services after disclosing sexual abuse by my father. I had to say goodbye to my family, my home, my friends, and my way of life. I cried. I was scared. I felt alone and depressed. But that was not the only time in my life that I had to say goodbye. There have been many situations and circumstances since. Goodbyes are part of the cycle of life. However, saying goodbye is not easy to do. So why is saying goodbye hard? Because it is upsetting, it signifies the end of a period of comfortability, the end of an era, a chapter in your life. It is awkward, scary, and causes fear.

Fearing the unknown. Dread the thought of starting again, or starting afresh, and the 'better stick with what I know' mentality. But you know that in order to live an empowered life – which is an important part of being exceptional and not expected – will call for some goodbyes: goodbye to old ways of doing things. Goodbye to people – this is not a negative thing: sometimes people outgrow each other. At times, people are only in your life for a reason or season. Other times, it's time to move on because the relationship has become toxic, and harmful. Also, saying goodbye to the old you to embrace the person you are evolving into. I am reminded of a bible scripture about new wine in old wineskins. *And no one puts new wine into old wineskins; or else the new wine bursts the wineskins, the wine is spilled, and the wineskins are ruined. But new wine must be put into new wineskins.* (**Mark 2:22**). You cannot be the old version and develop the new you at the same time. However, it is a translational journey. Going from the old to the new.

So how to recognise the sign it is time to say goodbye? Here are some things I've recognised from my experience:

It causes you more harm than good.

It no longer feels right.

You don't have any inner peace.

You know in your heart it is time to say goodbye, but do not know how to.

You are not growing, evolving, or becoming a better person with the thing you can't say goodbye to.

How to say goodbye

Do it in steps. Lessen contact, do it less, or do not indulge in it anymore; prise its fingers off your life.

Write down why it's beneficial to say goodbye to that thing.

Remind yourself of the positives and why they cannot come with you on your new journey. Remind yourself why 'hello' to the new thing is much more important than 'goodbye' to the old thing.

Complete this sentence. Saying goodbye to (put a name to it) will empower me, free me, help me to become a healthier person, make better choices, boost my confidence. If you remember the promise of the thing you want to say hello to, it will make the goodbye easier.

So, teach us to number our days, that we may gain a heart of wisdom. **Psalm 90:12**

Value Over Cost

There is a cost to living an empowered life; understanding the difference between cost and value, will either mean your life will move in a different direction or remain the same. Cost is not an issue when you understand the value of what you will gain, because you will see it as an investment. Personal intrinsic value is something that cannot be measured by money, but by things that are rewarding. It is crazy that people won't think twice about buying things they do not even want or need, but to spend twenty pounds on a self-help book, personal development, further education, or a therapy session, they consider the cost too much to spend. Yet they wonder why they remain stuck!

Purpose and career-wise, I am far from fulfilling and reaching my earning potential, yet I have always invested time and money in my development and the development of others. Because I understand the importance of intrinsic value, I have funded my non-profit for many years and invested in my empowerment company, therapy, books, and courses. I never consider the monetary cost, because I know the investment will pay off in the end. I also have the same mindset when it comes to paying people for their services. Along with everyone else, I do appreciate 'free' at times. However, I have no problem paying for things that will add value and benefit to me and the things that I am trying to build.

Value over cost has many benefits:

It maximises the things you want to do in your life.

It solves problems.

It brings breakthroughs and results.

It will help personal development.

It›s an investment in your future.

Think about stocks and shares. Investors make short, medium, and long-term investments. This is the same mindset you need to have towards your development. Understand that whatever the monetary cost, if you invest now, one day you will see a return.

If you want to get the best out of yourself, you must realise your value in every area of your life. Learn to adopt a future-thinking mindset, a mindset that is monetary and generous to self.

You shall sow you land for six years and gather in its yield. **Exodus 23:10**

Fear Requires You Live in Conformity Courage Frees You to Live Authentically

What's Your Next Step?

Are you the type of person who always thinks about the now? Do you ever have time to think about the next step in your life? The next thing you want to achieve?

Many people would say that thinking ahead is not appreciating the here and now. However, this is not true. I believe it is good to think about what you want to do next. It does not mean that you don›t appreciate your life currently. In my opinion, thinking about the next step is part of future planning. It is preparing to build upon your activities and achievements. It is the continuation of progress: having an eye on the future. I prepared for the next step in my life by understanding what I need to do to take it. I am studying for a master›s degree in Innovation Management and Entrepreneurship online. The course is part-time for two years. It is one of the most challenging things I have ever done. This is in addition to building my company, running a non-profit and looking after my family. However, for me, this is part of my next step, the progression of all I have achieved so far. This degree will enable me to develop my company, prepare me for opening my third business, and help me become a better entrepreneur.

The worst thing anyone can do is not have a plan or a vision for where they want to go. Therefore, the steps are crucial. It is not dismissive of what you are doing now – it is empowering you to prepare for the future. I want to share with you three benefits of planning your next step:

It gives you a blueprint to follow

Having a plan will help you decide upon the next step. You can plan what is needed for the next step in advance, rather than thinking about it on the spot.

Keeps you focused

The plan keeps you focused, but the steps keep you on track. Steps are the connector between where you are now and where you plan to be. It provides direction guiding you towards your goal.

Provides continuity

Taking steps builds consistency and continuity. Feed the feeling of progress and achievement. You may not yet have accomplished your end goal. However, with the continuity of taking steps, you will achieve it sooner than you think. Steps will lead you to your desired destination.

In my experience, I have found the next step is not revealed until you take the first one. Steps are there to help you feel that whatever you are trying to do is achievable. Use the method of taking steps to empower you to fulfil your goals, dreams, and aspirations, to help you to step forward with confidence. In doing so, you will be closer than you were yesterday.

A man›s heart devised his way: but the LORD directed his steps **Proverbs 16:9**

When Life Gives You Lemons

I have had a lot of lemons in my life. And just like the taste, for years, my life consisted of many sharp and bitter experiences. After a very long time I came to realise, that lemons, (those tough, horrible situations) can be turned into lemonade (situations to your advantage). Bad can be made into something good. Light can come from the darkness; you just need to find a way to turn those things designed to cause chaos, into positive power. The most recent lemon I tasted, was the Coronavirus pandemic. Indeed, most people on the planet had been handed this lemon. It affected everyone in some way or another; life as we know it, will never be the same again.

To have to deal with the sudden, unexpected changes it brought, has been challenging. For example, I must admit, the realisation of how the pandemic impacted my new-found business was difficult. But as time has passed (give or take a few up and down days), I have adapted to a new rhythm of life. As a matter of fact, during the lockdown, I used the time to work on and birth some amazing projects. I actively did things that further developed and strengthened me. I spent time with my family. I worked on my business. I finished outstanding work and created new products. I read great books and planned my next move. And amazingly, I developed and launched my first online course (the courage course) and finished my third book *Into the Unknown* which was published in November 2021.

I learned from this Coronavirus lemon, to make the most out of a bad situation. In general, I have learned from the lemons of life, that it is better to focus on the things I *can* change and do something about, rather than focus on things outside my control. I know in this new post-pandemic era, we are living in a fear that is ever-present concerning financial security and employment, amongst other things. But one thing life has taught me, is that you can add nothing to a situation by worrying. That doesn't mean I am immune to the worries of life, but I *choose* to remain optimistic. I hope and pray you can also do the same.

Do not let the lemons of life turn you bitter. Try and find a way to use negative or disempowering situations to your advantage and make lemonade by:

Staying Calm

Like the famous slogan 'keep calm and carry on'– do not panic. It will only make the situation worse. If you stay calm, you will be able to assess the situation better and notice something you did not consider before.

Do something different

Is there another way to deal with the challenge you are facing? How about approaching it in a different way? Sometimes the answer is right under your nose. It may not be obvious, especially when you have been used to doing things a certain way, or become used to the situation. Maybe it is time to consider a new thing. Maybe it is time to take a risk and give something else a try. What have you got to lose?

Talk to God

Just like you would talk with a friend. With God, all things are possible. He can make a way where there is no way.

Life will always bring the unexpected. However, you can choose to rise above its challenges in how you deal with them. You may surprise yourself and find that you exceed your own expectations. So today, I encourage you to make lemonade.

There is surely a future hope for you, and your hope will not be cut off. **Proverbs 23:18**

When People Have Low Expectations of You

Something that affected me over the years (well it did before, but not as much now) is the low expectation people had of me. Many things have contributed to people's low expectations of me: my dysfunctional behaviour after childhood abuse, my family background, and being brought up in the care system. I remember what was, at the time, a painful encounter with a fellow Christian woman who I saw years ago. I knew her years before that, as we were attending the same church. Back then, I was a young twenty-something, still in the midst of processing my trauma. I was suicidal and depressed; at the time she prayed for me and gave me moral support. The day I saw her again, was at a Christian women's conference that I was invited to as a speaker. I was no longer the broken woman that she once knew, instead, she saw an upbeat woman, now an author, speaker, and wife. I thought she would be glad to see that I made it through my challenges, but instead she said, 'oh are you still married?' with surprise in her voice. The look on her face and the tone of her voice told me all I needed to know. Her hurtful comments made me feel momentarily sad. But it was not the first or the last time that I would have this experience. Someone else, after I had come out of the hospital after I had a second mental health breakdown said, 'oh and the next time you go into hospital don't expect me to look after your daughter'. It was a wake-up call that I needed to turn my life around. People were waiting on my downfall.

My past life experiences and my outward troubles, had people believing the worst about me. To them, these were signs that I would not amount to anything in life. Low expectations had people who could not stand each other, come together to conspire, and destroy me and my family. Low expectations have caused people who I once loved, to do malicious things to me. These experiences have been hurtful, humiliating, disheartening, and discouraging. Had the Lord God not been on my side, I would have been destroyed and finished. People like the ones I have mentioned have a Barabbas mentality. Jesus was crucified by Pontius Pilate on the directive of a group of people because they hated the truth of his message. Instead, they voted to release Barabbas, a known criminal and murderer (Matthew:16-26). This mindset is prevalent in society today, where people want the worst for you. Many people would rather believe lowly of you, because they do not want you to prosper. They would rather believe the worst about you, even see you come to harm, break down or not do well. They would rather believe lies about you because they hate the truth; your natural progression in life is a problem. After all, it is not what they expected. Even though many people do not wish me well, I owed it to myself to succeed, be happy in my life and continue my journey to healing and loving myself. I live my life for myself, not for others.

If people have low expectations of you, it is because they see your potential. Maybe they hope that in voicing their low expectations of you, it will discourage you from attempting anything to further better or develop yourself. It is not nice when they voice their negativity to you. It is distasteful and disrespectful, but at least it shows you people's true colours. Look at the person, or people telling you this. What have they done with their life? That will tell you all that you need to know.

To deal with people's low expectations of you I would suggest you:

Rise above it.

Focus on you.

Do not live your life to please others.

Do not take their comments personally (when they project low expectations of you, they are dealing with low expectations of themselves).

Have high hopes for yourself.

If you have high hopes for yourself, that is all that matters. Remember, people do not have the final authority over your life – God does.

For I know the thoughts that I think toward you, says the Lord, thoughts of peace and not of evil, to give you a future and a hope **Jeremiah 29:11**

Why DO You do It?

Every now and then, I reflect on my transition from career to calling, via my charitable and business endeavours (Daughter Arise and YEME Empowerment). I realised from the twenty-three years that I worked in traditional employment, (working directly for a company as an employee) that I never asked myself the deeper question of *why* I did those jobs. At the time, I didn't think it mattered.

A lot of the decisions that I made up until the age of thirty-five years old, had very little to do with what I wanted in life. As a wife and mother, responsibilities overrode any desire I had to do anything that made *me* happy, or to follow my dreams. My decisions were heavily influenced by external factors. I had bills to pay. Childcare to pay for in order to go to work – and the list goes on and on. I lived my life at the mercy of circumstances – but making those decisions came at a cost. I was constantly stressed and unfulfilled, because I denied myself the opportunity to discover and explore my potential. I had no end goal and nothing to personally look forward to. I lived in a fog of uncertainty.

It was only when I discovered my purpose and calling in my mid-thirties, that I understood the importance of knowing the 'why' question. Now it's central to everything I do. It guides my choices and decisions, both in my personal life and business endeavours. Every decision I make regarding my family, my creative process, the videos I make, the blogs and books I write, the talks I give to empower people, the products I create – I know the reason why. Nothing is meaningless.

But now that I am older and wiser, I believe as we journey through this precious thing called life, it is important to ask yourself, *why* you do the thing you do.

If you haven›t asked yourself the ‹why› question, maybe it›s time to. You might be surprised at the revelations it brings. Here is how you can explore the why question:

If the reason *why* you do it is to please others, ask yourself, why does what *they* want matter more than your freedom to choose what *you* want to do with your life? Why did you give yourself so little power and say in your own life?

If what you are doing is solely to pay bills, or because it's comfortable or convenient, then why have you allowed these factors to determine you?

If you know you are not living to your full potential and sense you are doing things below your capability and potential, why have you allowed or made decisions that underestimate or devalue, you?

God has given you life to bring him glory through your skills, talents, and experiences. Even if you do not acknowledge God in your life his gifts are without repentance *(Romans 11:29)*. To live in less than the fullness of his purpose four your life is short-changing yourself.

Now is the time to flip the why. If you have goals, dreams, or desire to do something different why not do it? Don't give yourself excuses why it can't be done. You won't know until you give it a try. Now is the time to go for what you want. Why not?

The thief's purpose is to steal and kill and destroy. My purpose is to give them a rich and satisfying life. **John 10:10**

Why Are You Stuck

I have noticed in my work as an empowerment coach, that in my conversations with my clients, they all have in common the desire to want to do something different. However, they find themselves stuck. Some of them cited the reasons they are stuck, as being because of the people they hang around or associate with. Past experiences keep them bound (you'd be surprised – or maybe not – by how past experiences such as trauma, fear, and rejection have a long-lasting impact). Inherited generational mindset (people within the family only getting to a certain point in life, and not seeing any examples of family members that have gone further). Not being able to change or adapt. No plan, goal purpose, fear, comfort, and lack of courage. As you can see, many things keep people stuck!

There was a long period in my life where I was stuck with one thing or another. Trauma had me stuck. Depression had me stuck. How I viewed myself had me stuck, and circumstances (jobs, finances) had me stuck. Let me tell you, being stuck sucks! How I became *un*stuck started with a decision and a desire for change. That first decision was the hardest decision to make, because I realised my excuses were enabling me to remain in a stuck place. The desire came first and then action (dealing with habits, and issues). Oh, and also to *believe* there was hope for me. The belief that Jesus through His Holy Spirit could transform my life and help me become unstuck. The belief that being stuck is not who I am; just a culmination of things that have happened to me along the way that I could not get out of. You see, really that is the starting point of becoming unstuck: The desire to want change. The desire to want to overcome whatever you're facing or what has hindered you. To no longer settle for less. To want more. To be curious about exploring your potential. To explore life differently.

Some of you reading this entry probably realise you›ve been stuck for a long time. Some of you may be scared because you realise you have been in this place of ‹stuckness' (I know that is probably not a word) and in the same place you were, one, five, or even a decade ago. It has probably dawned on you, that the gift of time is moving on, but you are standing still. Before I share a few tips about how to start becoming unstuck, I want to encourage you to not lose hope in yourself or make your constant battle with being stuck in a particular area of your life break you down. There is a saying: *when you know better you do better.* Sometimes, being stuck simply comes from not knowing how to become unstuck, or not seeing anyone around you become unstuck in their circumstances or experiences. You wonder 'if could just' ... (fill in the blank). However, if some of you are honest with yourself, being stuck is a place of comfort, because it requires nothing from you, so you remain there. But in all circumstances, there is hope. To become unstuck, you must:

Desire change

You can become unstuck. You just need to desire to want change, believe it can happen and get support to do the work. Think about the things you desire more than remaining stuck. Use whatever it is as your motivation.

Identify what you are stuck with

Take some time to reflect and be honest with yourself. What is keeping you stuck?

Think about what will help you become unstuck

As mentioned already, sometimes the thing you are stuck with can be deep-rooted. In those circumstances, seeking professional support from a therapist might help start the journey to becoming unstuck. If the cause has its origins in habits or comfort, write down at least one thing that is opposite to what you usually do in your 'stuck' routine. Try and start to break the pattern. Find help and act to loosen the knots, to become *unstuck*.

Remember, stuck is not who you are. Don't let it become your identity. Today, you can start the journey of becoming unstuck if you desire to.

Now the Lord is the Spirit; and where the Spirit of the Lord is, there is liberty **(2 Corinthians 3:17)**

You Are a Uniquely Special Person

God created you to be one of a kind; you are a unique and special person. Your uniqueness can inspire, influence, and help someone else; it is your Unique Selling Point.

Sometimes, it can be difficult to recognise and stand in our uniqueness, especially when we live in a world that encourages us to fit in. Often, having an opinion different from other people's can put you on dangerous ground. Cancel culture is real. Even so, you must embrace everything that makes you unique; your beliefs, the way you do things, and what you stand for – all of you.

I used to struggle with embracing who I was. Throughout my life, people commented that I am complex, difficult to understand and strong-minded. These comments were made as negatives about me. At the time when I was experiencing these comments, I thought there was something wrong with me. I suffered from low self-esteem and confidence, and those comments caused me to be harsh and unaccepting of myself. However, as I have got older, grown in confidence, and embraced myself wholeheartedly, I see the way I am as a blessing. It is good to be different. If you struggle with embracing your uniqueness, I want to share with you tips on how to start getting comfortable being you:

Embrace yourself

The most crucial step is to accept you. <u>**ALL OF YOU**</u>. **Your quirks, traits, and personality**. Don't reject any part of you. When you start from that standpoint, you can then work on yourself if you choose to.

Don't compare yourself to others

To compare is impairing. When you compare yourself to other people, you diminish who you are and what you have to offer. You damage and limit your potential and weaken your position, opening the door for fear, jealousy, and insecurity to creep in. Never measure yourself against someone else's looks, abilities, or accomplishments. Appreciate you.

Identify your skills and talents

In doing so, you will strengthen your individual value both internally and externally. Furthermore, when you discover your life purpose, and you connectively interweave this into all aspects of your life, it will enhance your skills and talents – because you have found the power to be who you really are everything works in harmony.

Work on self-esteem and confidence issues

You can do this through therapy or trying new and different things. You must replace the old way of viewing yourself with new beliefs and perspectives and change your mindset.

The key is to be true to yourself. Do not feel insecure about who you are. Share your uniqueness with those around you what you have to offer is valuable and different. Don't be afraid of being unique – you are God's masterpiece.

I will praise You, for I am fearfully and wonderfully made; Marvellous are Your works, and that my soul knows very well **Psalm 139:14**

You are Worth Your Weight in GOLD

In this material-obsessed world, where success is measured by the acquirement of things, titles, and money, it can be easy to forget that *you* and not *things* are the real prize. **Evidence of your worth and wealth is not found outside of you; it's what's in you that is worth more than its weight in gold.**

I want to remind you of your preciousness by sharing these affirmations to encourage you:

What you have is more valuable than money.

You possess knowledge, skills and experiences that can influence your family, friends, community, and the world.

You have the power to create change.

You can help people.

You can teach them what you know.

No one can do what you do or bring what you can.

You are valuable. Therefore, add value to anything you create or contribute to.

Gold can never be eroded, tarnished, or diminished. Just like your skills, talents and experiences, who you are can never be taken away from you. They are God-given and can only be developed and enhanced further with time. Nothing in the eyes of others can diminish your value. Not riches, status, or anything else.

To discover and develop your gold you need to:

Know your identity and walk in it.

Find your purpose and live in it.

Spend time developing your skills and talents.

Find your tribe and share your knowledge and experiences and empower them.

You are God's creation. If you call on the name of God, he will open your eyes to more than you can ask, think, or imagine. About you, your life, and your place in this world.

Remember you are GOLD!

And you shall remember the Lord your God, for it is He who gives you power to get wealth, that He may establish His covenant which He swore to your fathers, as it is this day. **Deuteronomy 8:18**

SALVATION PRAYER

If you want to live an empowered life to be exceptional and not expected, God can empower you to live that life. Go to him as you are, share your heart with him and trust him to lead you on the right part. The prayer below is for you.

Dear Lord Jesus,

I am sorry for the things I have done wrong in my life. I ask your forgiveness. Thank you for dying on the cross for me to set me free from my sins. Please come into my life and fill me with your Holy Spirit and be with me forever. Empower me to live my life to the full through your Holy Spirit. Thank you, Lord Jesus, Amen.

Do you need a courageous action plan to achieve your goals and dreams? Check out The Courage Course on Thinkific.com
https://theempoweredlife-ad5c.thinkific.com/courses/the-courage-course

Social media:
YouTube – Living the Empowered Life
Instagram – Yeme_Empowerment
Twitter – Yeme Empowerment
Facebook – Yeme Empowerment
Tik Tok – yeme_empowerment22

Visit www.yemeempowerment.com to see what services and resources we offer for solutions to your current challenges.

Also, you can check out the Living the Empowered Life Podcast on Apple iTunes, Stitcher, and Spotify.

Get in touch. I would love to connect with you!